QUICK & EASY
HOME DECORATING

SUCCESSFUL PROJECTS STEP-BY-STEP

CREATIVE
HOME
ARTS
—CLUB—

Minnetonka, Minnesota

QUICK & EASY HOME DECORATING
SUCCESSFUL PROJECTS STEP-BY-STEP

Printed in 2005.

Published by North American Membership Group under license from International Masters Publishers, Inc.

Tom Carpenter
Creative Director

Heather Koshiol
Managing Editor

Michele Stockham
Senior Book Development Coordinator

Jenya Prosmitsky
Book Design & Production

Laura Holle
Assistant Book Development Coordinator

4 5 6 7 / 07 06 05

ISBN 1-58159-205-1
© 2003 Creative Home Arts Club

Creative Home Arts Club
12301 Whitewater Drive
Minnetonka, MN 55343
www.creativehomeartsclub.com

CONTENTS

INTRODUCTION

Welcome to
QUICK & EASY HOME DECORATING

Your guide to
SUCCESSFUL PROJECTS STEP-BY-STEP

Decorating should never be a chore. Creating the projects you will use to improve and enhance the look of your home should be a fun and enjoyable endeavor. And in today's busy world, that means both "quick" and "easy."

Those are the simple ideas behind *Quick & Easy Home Decorating*.

Every time you turn a page, you're going to discover a new and exciting home decorating project that you can create easily and affordably. This book is literally packed cover-to-cover with ideas!

A great photo displays each completed project so you can see how it should look. Step-by-step pictures show you exactly how to create each idea efficiently and effectively … on your budgets of time *and* money.

You will also find lists of materials and tools you will need, detailed templates and diagrams, handy hints to help you along, dollar-saving ideas, "oops" tips in case you make mistakes, crafting notes and tips, quick fixes and more.

Start with your "windows of decorating opportunity." Then give old pieces of furniture a second chance. Don't forget about your walls, doors and floors. Create storage space that offers real style too. And take advantage of the power of flowers.

Those are the kinds of ideas you'll find on the upcoming pages. So let's get going. It's time to do some *Quick & Easy Home Decorating*!

CREATIVE
HOME
ARTS
—CLUB—

WINDOWS
OF OPPORTUNITY

*Windows present some of a home's most
intriguing decorating possibilities. Every
"livable" room has at least one window.
And any window is a focal point because of
the life-giving light that streams through.
You can decorate a window by framing it
(with curtains, drapes, specialty frames),
covering it (with accented blinds and rollers)
or even decorating the pane itself (with
paint or etching). Here are plenty of ideas—
quick and easy to create, of course—on
what to do with all your windows of
opportunity.*

WHIMSICAL DRAPERY TACKS

Personalize your windows inexpensively with drapery tacks.

YOU WILL NEED

❏ SMALL WOODEN SHELLS
❏ PUSH PINS
❏ GLUE GUN & GLUE STICKS
❏ PAINTS
❏ PAINTBRUSH
❏ PENCIL
❏ STRAIGHTEDGE

8

BEFORE YOU BEGIN

Potential ornaments for drapery tacks can be found all around your home. Here are a few suggestions, plus some pointers to help you secure your tacks.

Securing the Tacks

Lightly tapping the head of the push pin with a hammer will help the pins drive straight into the wood. Don't tap too hard, or the head is liable to break off the pin.

For extra security, dab a bit of clear-drying glue onto the placement mark before pushing in the pin. This will give the tack additional support.

For push pins used on drywall, apply glue to the placement mark, then press the pin firmly into the wall. Use a hammer only if the pin won't go through the drywall.

If necessary, glue a small cardboard circle to the pin head, then glue the decorative item to the circle. This will give you a greater surface area on which to glue the ornament.

Choosing Items

By using a little imagination, just about any small item can be put to good use as an ornament on a drapery tack.
• For a nursery window, glue some small building blocks to the ends of the tacks.

• For a bedroom window, choose pretty silk flower heads that complement the decor of the room.

• For a casual kitchen window, keep your eyes open for tiny knives, forks or spoons.

MAKING THE DRAPERY TACKS

HANDY HINTS

Using drapery tacks allows you to change your window treatment in mere minutes. Just pull out the tacks, change the decorative fronts, then gather and fold your new curtain fabric and tack into place.

A yard of fabric is all you need for a valance to use with drapery tacks. For longer curtains, use more fabric.

1 Use a paintbrush to paint the wooden shells on one side. When the paint is dry, turn the shell over and paint the other side. If desired, add highlights in another color.

2 Use a straightedge and pencil to measure and mark the placement of each tack. Make sure the tacks are evenly spaced, with enough room between for the shell to lie flat.

3 Use a push pin to hold one top corner of the curtain in place on the first pencil mark. Gather soft folds along the top of the curtain and continue pinning it in place on the pencil marks until the other end of the curtain is reached. Stand back and ensure the drapes in the curtain are falling equally.

4 Using a glue gun, carefully coat the end of one push pin with hot glue, then press a shell firmly onto the pin head. Hold the shell in place for at least two minutes to allow the glue to dry. Continue adding shells to each of the remaining drapery tacks.

THE LOOK OF STAINED GLASS

Bathe a room in colored light by painting a stained glass window.

10

BEFORE YOU BEGIN

Paint a personalized pattern onto a window, then enjoy the beauty of stained glass. Because paint is not permanent, it will require touch-ups over time.

Preparing the Window

It is easier to work on a flat surface, so remove the window, if possible.

To remove the window from the frame, use a putty knife to pry away old putty (right). Take out the glazier points and remove the glass from the frame.

Clean the window thoroughly. Remove dirt and grease with a lint-free cloth.

If it is necessary to paint the window while it is still in the frame, protect the wood with masking tape and take care that the paint does not run or drip.

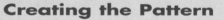

Creating the Pattern

To use this template, or any design of your choice, enlarge the design on a photocopier to fit the window. Once the proportions are right, place the design under the glass if you are working flat, or tape it to the back of the window if you are working vertically. Make sure the design side is facing up.

Use a marking pen that will write on any surface, or use simulated liquid leading to trace the design directly onto the window.

CREATING FAUX STAINED GLASS

1 Remove window pane and clean it thoroughly. Position paper pattern under window pane. Use simulated liquid leading to outline pattern. Try not to cross over previously drawn lines at intersections.

2 Remove paper pattern and examine outlining. Pop any air bubbles with a pin. Allow leading to dry for at least eight hours, then use a craft knife to trim away any thick patches, particularly at intersecting lines.

3 Working from interior out toward edges, start filling in design. Use darkest paint color first and complete one color before moving on to next.

4 Fill in remaining colors, using a toothpick where necessary to fill in corners. Use a generous amount of paint, and smooth, rather than stroke, it onto window; brush strokes will blend as paint dries.

5 Let window dry overnight. Touch up design as required. To reinstall pane, slip glazier points into channel between glass and frame; tap with a hammer until sharp edge penetrates frame by $1/8$ to $1/4$ inch.

6 Use a putty knife to add caulk around edges of window pane to secure it in frame. This simulated stained glass technique is only suitable for interior windows and should not be used on windows that are subjected to excessive moisture or humidity. To clean painted windows, wipe with a soft, dry cloth. Do not spray window cleaner directly onto painted glass.

CREATIVE WINDOW DRAFT STOPPERS

Keep your room warm with unique, decorative draft stoppers.

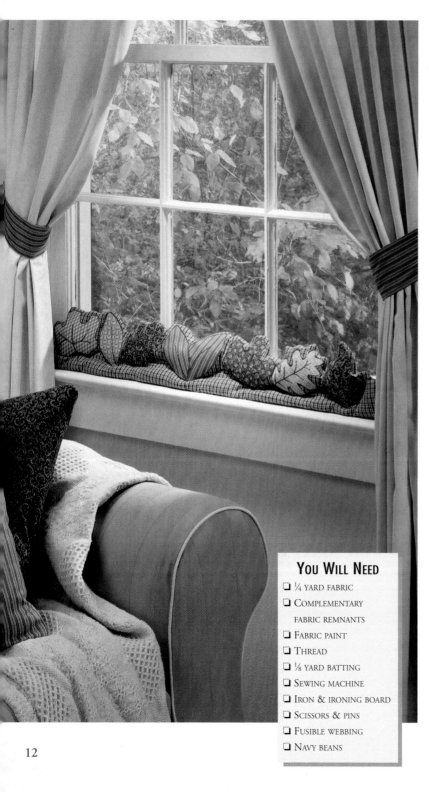

BEFORE YOU BEGIN

Fabric appliqués and fabric paint turn an ordinary draft stopper into a unique design feature. Choose a theme and fabric to match the decor of the room.

Preparing the Materials

Enlarge the leaf patterns (below) on a photocopier to desired size; leaves should be approximately 4 to 5 inches high. Cut out each leaf to make a template. Iron fusible webbing onto the back sides of fabric remnants. Then draw around templates onto webbing side of remnants; cut out two or three copies of each leaf.

To mark the position of leaves on the main fabric, fold fabric in half widthwise with right sides together.

Position paper templates of leaves in desired positions along top edge of fabric. Use a fabric marking pen to roughly outline the basic shapes of the leaves.

The dimensions of the draft stopper should be as follows: Length of tube = 2 inches longer than windowsill width from one inner frame edge to the other. Width of tube = 16 inches. Batting = Same length as fabric and 5 inches wide.

MAKING THE DRAFT STOPPER

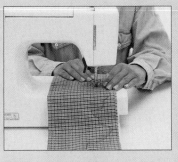

1 With right sides facing, fold fabric rectangle in half to bring long edges together. Pin batting between layers to align with top edge. Batting will extend two-thirds down height of fabric.

2 Use a running stitch to sew through all three layers down one short side and along length of fabric, following outline of top of leaves. Make sure stitches do not extend below bottom of batting.

3 Cut through all three layers close to stitching. If seam allowance feels bulky, trim batting even closer to stitching. Turn tube right side out; press.

4 Place fabric leaves in position on front of tube, ½ inch in from top edge. Make sure each leaf aligns with its corresponding outline. Fuse in place, following manufacturer's instructions.

5 To form a tube to hold beans, machine stitch ½ inch away from bottom edge of leaves, following outlines. Make sure stitches catch bottom edge of batting.

6 Use fabric paint to outline edges of leaves and highlight inner details. To prevent smudges, begin painting in center and work toward edges.

7 Fill tube at bottom of draft stopper with dried beans, periodically shaking the tube to disperse them evenly; do not overfill. When satisfied with weight of draft stopper, turn in raw edges of opening, then hand or machine stitch opening closed. Place finished draft stopper on windowsill against bottom of window.

PAINTED BLINDS FOR AN OUTDOOR VIEW

Delight passersby with a fun design on the outside of blinds.

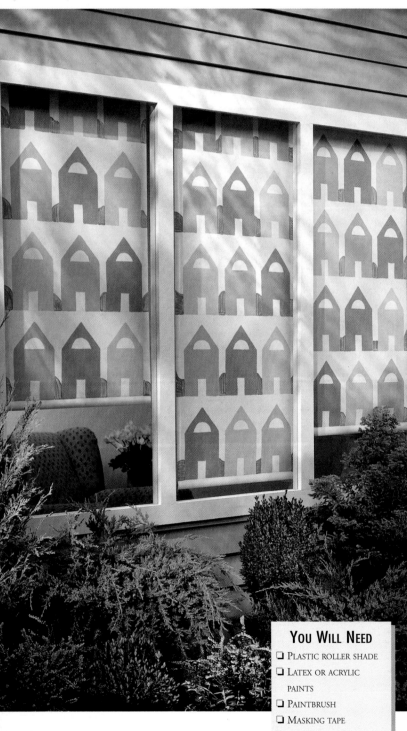

BEFORE YOU BEGIN

Roller blinds are an easy and inexpensive way to add a decorative touch to the outside view of your home.

Planning the Design

Plan the design to complement the outside of the house.

Single windows are easiest to plan since the design needs only to work on its own.

Multiple windows require careful planning since the design must look good on the collective grouping as well as on the independent window. It is also important that the design maintains its appeal when the blinds are set at varying heights.

Use a blackout blind so that the design won't show through on the other side. If it will show through, choose a design that will work well as a mirror image, and then trace and paint it on the inside.

There are many design sources to use as inspiration. Copy a design from wallpaper, then enlarge it on a photocopier to fit the shade. Alternatively, paint a freehand design, planning it first on a piece of paper that is the same size as the shade. Precut stencils are another good design source. Use them on their own or combined with your own ideas.

Measure the blind, then enlarge or reduce the template (bottom) on a photocopier so that the houses will fill the whole space vertically and horizontally (below).

Trace the outline of the house onto heavy paper and use it as a template to draw around.

PAINTING THE SHADE

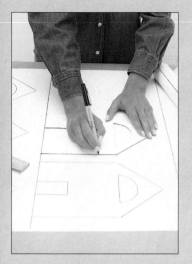  

HANDY HINTS

It is just as easy to paint fabric shades. Plan the design in the same way, and mark it directly on the fabric with a fabric marking pen. Use fabric paints to create the design, and apply fabric stiffener to the shade after it has been painted.

1 Once size of template has been determined, use pencil and T square to mark horizontal and vertical placement lines on blind. Draw around template to copy house design onto blind.

2 Apply long vertical strips of painter's masking tape just inside outline of houses from top to bottom of shade. Apply horizontal strips of masking tape outside placement line at bottom of houses.

3 Use a pencil or felt tip pen to mark outline of grassy mound between houses. Use a foam brush to fill in grassy area with green paint. Allow paint to dry completely, then remove strips of masking tape.

4 Apply new strips of masking tape to outside edges of houses to protect green painted area and area below houses. Use a foam brush to fill in outlines of houses in alternating colors; leave doors and windows white, or paint in a different color if desired. Allow paint to dry completely before removing masking tape and hanging blind.

ROLLER BLINDS WITH HEM APPEAL

Make any window a point of interest with trimmed roller blinds.

BEFORE YOU BEGIN

Make a one-of-a-kind roller blind to dress up any window. The customized hem is deceptively simple, yet dramatic and appealing.

Choosing Roller Blind Fabric

Besides matching your decor, the fabric for a roller blind should block light. Look for a medium-to-heavyweight weave.
• To determine how much fabric to buy, measure the window inside the frame. Add 8 inches to the length and 1 inch to the width.
• Purchase lining material at one third the length and the same width as the roller blind fabric.

Pointers for Zigzags

To make the zigzags along the bottom of the blind, determine the number of points desired. Then divide the width of the window by the number of zigzags.

To make a template, draw one zigzag in the correct proportion on a piece of cardboard and cut it out. Lay the template on the fabric and trace, repeating the design across the entire bottom of the shade.

Roller Blind Hardware

Attach the brackets on the inside of the window using a screwdriver (below).

Measure the distance between the brackets to determine the dowel's length. Place a cap on the end of the dowel, insert pin and gently hammer into place.

The slotted bracket (1) goes on the left side of the window; the round bracket (2) is for the right side.

MAKING A ZIGZAG ROLLER BLIND

1 Cut blind and lining fabrics (Before You Begin). Using template, mark hem design on wrong side of fabric. Stitch lining and fabric, right sides facing, along lines. Trim seams and points, clip corners; turn.

2 Turn under long edge of lining; slipstitch to blind. To make casing, draw a line across blind 1½ inches above points. Draw a parallel line, 1½ inches above first; stitch along lines. Open seam at each end of casing.

3 Following manufacturer's instructions, apply liquid seam protector to raw edges on each side of blind to prevent fraying edges. Let dry. Turn sides under ½ inch and press; stitch close to inner edge.

5 Install hardware to inside of window frame (Before You Begin), making sure rod sits close to top edge of frame and hangs nicely. Make certain that rod ends match hardware openings. Then, attach blind to rod with masking tape along back edge of rod. Hang rod and fix blind length in window.

4 Using matching thread, hand stitch jingle bell to end of each hem point. Secure each bell by knotting thread on back of blind. Cut thread ends close to stitching.

DECORATIVE WINDOW FRAMES

Frame a window with original art using stencils and colorful paint.

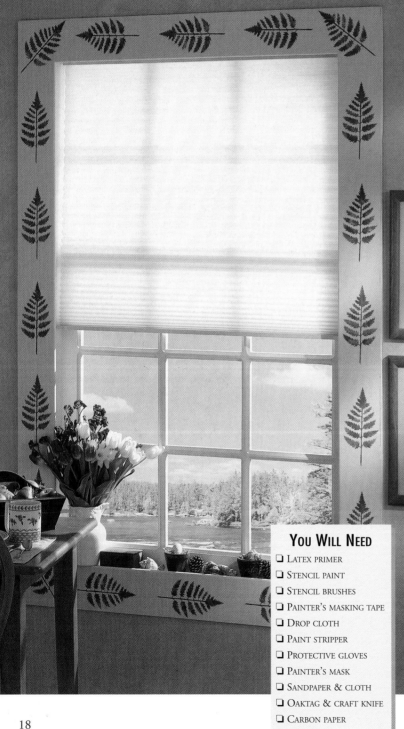

YOU WILL NEED

- ❏ LATEX PRIMER
- ❏ STENCIL PAINT
- ❏ STENCIL BRUSHES
- ❏ PAINTER'S MASKING TAPE
- ❏ DROP CLOTH
- ❏ PAINT STRIPPER
- ❏ PROTECTIVE GLOVES
- ❏ PAINTER'S MASK
- ❏ SANDPAPER & CLOTH
- ❏ OAKTAG & CRAFT KNIFE
- ❏ CARBON PAPER

BEFORE YOU BEGIN

Inspect your window frames. It may be necessary to remove old layers of paint before applying new primer and topcoat, and beginning to stencil.

Preparing a Window Frame

Cover the area under the window with a drop cloth or newspaper to catch any paint spills.

Cover the window itself with paper, or apply painter's masking tape to the glass along the edge of the frame to protect it from paint spills or splashes.

Wear rubber gloves and a painter's mask and work in a well-ventilated area.

Follow the manufacturer's instructions and apply the paint stripper to the window molding. The thicker the stripper consistency, the easier it will be to work with on a vertical surface.

Remove all paint from the grooves and details of the frame. Use a sponge and clear water to carefully rinse the frame. Allow the frame to dry thoroughly.

Cutting a Template

Enlarge the leaf template (below) on a photocopier to the desired size or trace it onto graph paper to a finished size of 8½ by 4½ inches.

Cut an oaktag strip the width of the window frame molding by 11 inches long. Transfer one leaf design to

the oaktag strip using carbon paper and pencil.

Cut out the fern leaf stencil using a sharp craft knife. Be careful around the margins of the leaflets. It may be necessary to trace the leaf more than once with the knife to get a clean cut.

STENCILING A WINDOW FRAME

1 Lightly sand window frame until surface is smooth. Wipe clean with tack cloth to remove any traces of dust and grit left from paint residue and sanding. Window frame is now ready for primer coat.

2 Using a 2-inch trim brush, apply wood primer to stripped window frame, painting in direction of wood grain. Primer helps paint adhere to wood. Allow primer to dry; check manufacturer's directions.

3 Lightly sand primed window frame smooth. Carefully clean sanded surface with tack cloth. Paint window frame with topcoat of paint; allow to dry. Lightly sand and apply topcoat again, if necessary.

HANDY HINTS

To control the paint when stenciling, dip the tip of the stencil brush in paint. Blot the brush onto a paper towel until the bristles are almost dry, then apply the paint.

TAKE NOTE

Paint stripper can be toxic. Cover your hands and arms and wear a painter's mask before you start to work.

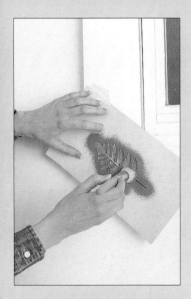

4 Mark placement for stencils around window frame. Position stencil on lower corner of frame. Secure with painter's masking tape. Work in circular motion, pouncing brush within stencil to apply paint.

5 Carefully lift painter's masking tape and stencil card from frame and stencil single fern leaf diagonally across three remaining corners. Allow paint to dry completely. Place stencil card on upper frame and tape down at marked point near previously painted corner leaf; paint. Repeat painting procedure around entire frame. Walls may be painted before or after stenciling project.

ONE-OF-A-KIND WINDOW BORDERS

Make your own stamps to create enticing window borders in no time.

BEFORE YOU BEGIN

Use easy-to-make print blocks to create a unique, stamped border around a window.

Making a Stamp Block

On a photocopier, enlarge the templates (below) approximately 100%. Trace each design onto tracing paper. Mark the top of each tracing with an "X".

Cut wood blocks slightly larger than the designs (approximately 5 by 5 inches). Mark the top of each block with an "X".

Use carbon paper to transfer the designs to the backs of pressure-sensitive foam sheets. Cut out with scissors or a craft knife.

Peel the paper backing from the cutout foam designs. Press each foam shape firmly to the back of a wood block. To provide a reference point when stenciling, glue the tracing paper design to the top side of each block, matching the "X" marks on the tracings with those on the blocks.

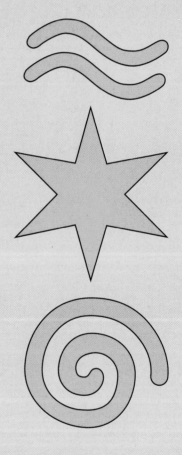

Stamp Pads

Rather than applying paint onto the stamp with a small roller or paintbrush, make a felt stamp pad.
• Cut one 5- by 5-inch felt square for each paint color being used.

• Add a small amount of paint extender to the color and mix well. Wearing rubber gloves, place the felt square in the paint to soak.
• Once the felt square is saturated, transfer it to a disposable, plastic tray.

STAMPING WINDOW BORDERS

1 Mark a border, 5 inches out from frame, with masking tape. Measure frame to determine number of designs that will fit. Starting at bottom, mark first placement with pencil. Continue around frame, spacing evenly.

2 Apply gold acrylic paint to stamp with small roller or paintbrush. Apply paint thinly and evenly over entire surface area of stamp, or press stamp on felt pad (Before You Begin). Reapply paint for each use.

3 Position stamp between tape and frame, aligning block with first pencil mark; press firmly against wall. Alternate and rotate designs while moving from mark to mark for different effects.

HANDY HINTS

If the print block is sliding, there is too much paint on the stamp. Blot excess paint onto a piece of paper before stamping.

TAKE NOTE

Clean each stamp block immediately after use. Do not soak them: With warm, soapy water, gently scrub the blocks with a soft toothbrush.

4 Touch up any lightly stamped areas using a small paintbrush. Fill in special details and accents at end. If you want variations in color, try layering light-colored shapes under dark ones, or simultaneously apply two or more colors of paint to stamp block.

A GREAT WINDOW GREENHOUSE

Add a flourish to any room with a pretty window garden.

YOU WILL NEED

- ❑ 1- BY 6-INCH WHITE PINE
- ❑ ⅜-INCH SISAL ROPE & ⅛-INCH TWINE
- ❑ HAND DRILL & PADDLE DRILL BIT
- ❑ SCREW EYES
- ❑ WOOD STAIN
- ❑ PAINTBRUSH
- ❑ TAPE MEASURE
- ❑ LIGHT SANDPAPER
- ❑ GLUE GUN & GLUE STICKS

BEFORE YOU BEGIN

The basic ingredients are simple, but the effect is quite stunning. Match a wood stain to the existing window or paint the shelf in a contrasting color.

Planning and Preparing

To determine the number of shelves and their sizes, measure the height (a), width (b) and depth (c) of the inside of the window casing. (See diagram below.)

• To determine the spacing between the shelves, measure the height of the potted plants and add 1 to 2 inches for "breathing room." A small window will accommodate two to three shelves. A large window looks more balanced with an odd number of shelves.

• From a 1- by 6-inch, or narrower if necessary, piece of white pine or other soft wood, cut three shelves ¾ inch shorter than the width of the window. For a small charge, a lumberyard will precut the shelves.

• With fine-grade sandpaper, sand the top, bottom and ends of the wood shelves. Clean the surface using a soft cloth.

• Using utility scissors, cut four pieces of ⅜-inch natural sisal rope the height of the window opening, plus 25 inches—5 inches for each knot, plus 5 inches at each of the top and bottom shelves for looping through the screw eyes. Cut eight pieces of matching twine 30 inches long, to allow for wrapping the rope 12 times and for tucking the ends to secure.

• To prevent the wood from warping, place the vertical sisal supports every 30 inches or less to properly support the weight of the plants. For example, if a window measures more than 36 inches wide, add two ropes in the center of the window shelves and loop through the screw eyes.

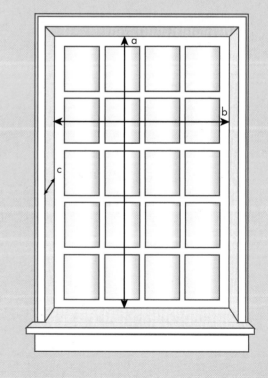

MAKING THE WINDOW GREENHOUSE

1 Measure 3 inches from each end and 1 inch from the front and back edges of the shelves; mark with a pencil. Using a power drill and a ½-inch paddle drill bit, drill four holes in each shelf. Finely sand the holes to smooth them.

2 Choose a stain to match or coordinate with the decor. With a foam brush, apply stain to the top, bottom and edges of the shelves. Lightly sand and reapply stain. Finish with a coat of polyurethane.

3 Starting at the bottom of the rope, take the distance from the sill to the first shelf, add 5 inches and tie knots. Slip the ropes up through the shelf holes. Repeat measuring and knotting for all the shelves, adding 5 inches at the top.

4 Drill holes in the top and bottom window casings 3⅜ inches in from the sides and 1 inch in from the front and back of the casing. Install screw eyes that are large enough for the sisal rope to slip through easily.

5 Put the rope ends through the top screw eyes. Loop the ropes down next to themselves for 5 inches. Knot twine around the sisal, then wrap tightly about 12 times. Tuck the ends in and hot-glue to secure.

6 Carefully check the level of all the shelves and adjust the top knots, if necessary. Next, loop the ropes through the screw eyes up next to themselves at the bottom of the casing for 5 inches and repeat wrapping and securing with the twine. Glue the ends of all the wrapped ropes. Allow the ends to dry and then check that they are properly glued.

DRESSED UP
WINDOW BLINDS

Add color and pattern to give old blinds a new image.

BEFORE YOU BEGIN

Painting a metal or plastic mini-blind is an inexpensive way to add character and charm to a room. A little paint, two or three sponges and a bit of artistry does the trick.

Planning the Design

With an existing blind, dip it in a tub of sudsy water and lightly scrub it with a brush; rinse. Let it dry thoroughly before painting. Mini-blinds with a matte finish are the easiest to use and need very little preparation. Paints are less likely to stick to a glossy surface, so lightly sand the surface before applying the paint.

Look for design ideas that are simple shapes with soft edges. Avoid straight or angled edges and geometrics. Study cloud formations and keep sketches (below) of interesting shapes and formations.

Plan the design on paper first. Measure the blind and transfer the dimensions to a piece of ¼-inch graph paper. Draw a small diagram of the general placement of the cloud forms. Fill the entire space of the blind with formations.

Indicate the lighter highlights on top and darker shadows on the bottom of the clouds.

The Materials

Sponges and paints are the only materials necessary to produce this soft technique.
• Use regular bottled acrylic craft paint in white and blue.

• Experiment with sponge textures. Sea sponges produce large, dense and fluffy designs. Cellulose sponges create smaller patterns, perfect for painting the shadows under the clouds.

PAINTING THE BLIND

1 Lay the blind flat on top of a covered table and adjust the slats evenly. Using drafting tape, tape the slats together along the outside edges of the blind to prevent them from moving during painting process.

2 Using a soft lead pencil and following the scaled diagram (Before You Begin), outline the general shapes of the cloud forms onto the face of the blind. For realism, emphasize the central mass of each cloud.

3 Wet a sea sponge with water and squeeze it out. Dip in white paint and sponge in the central areas of each cloud. Blend out over the pencil markings to soften the edges and give a natural appearance.

HANDY HINTS

Always test the effects of a particular sponge on paper before applying it to the blind. Cut and reshape a sponge for the desired results. Experiment with the amount of paint used. Mix paint colors and use more than two colors, if desired.

DOLLAR SENSE

Save plastic and foam meat trays, take-out food containers and other flat, shallow receptacles with slightly raised edges to recycle and use as paint trays.

4 Using the same sponge (rinse with clear water to clean) or different sponge textures, apply the second coat of blue paint. Stand back and look at the overall effect and add white or blue spongings to the weakest areas. Erase any visible pencil marks.

DECORATIVE MOLDING FOR A WINDOW

Decorative molding adds easy, classic styling to any window.

YOU WILL NEED

- ❏ DECORATIVE MOLDING
- ❏ WOOD ADHESIVE
- ❏ CAULKING GUN
- ❏ LATEX PAINTER'S CAULK
- ❏ #8 FINISHING NAILS
- ❏ SAW & HAMMER
- ❏ LATEX PAINT & PAINTBRUSH
- ❏ FINE SANDPAPER
- ❏ WOOD PUTTY

BEFORE YOU BEGIN

The amazing variety of decorative moldings makes them perfect for adding interest to any window.

Using Corner Blocks

Decorative corner pieces are a natural way to finish a rectangular window.
• Purchase four separate motifs, such as these rosettes. Attach them in the corners of the window with wood adhesive.
• Cut strips of molding to fit between the blocks. Attach the strips with wood adhesive and finishing nails.

Mitering Corners

A miter box is invaluable when cutting angles. To form a perfect corner, measure four lengths of molding, allowing extra for mitering. Put one strip in miter box and cut each end through the 45° slot; repeat with remaining strips. Sand any rough spots. Check that all molding strips fit snugly at corners before fixing in place.

Removing Old Molding

Since molding is held in place with adhesive and finishing nails, it is relatively easy to remove. Slide a putty knife or paint scraper under the old molding and gently pry it free. Be careful the knife doesn't slip and damage the surrounding walls.

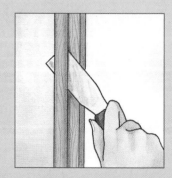

ADDING MOLDING TO A WINDOW

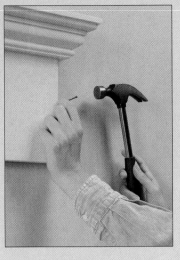

1 Mark placement of header molding over window. Lightly sand back of molding; apply wood adhesive along back with caulking gun, moving gun steadily along molding to form an even bead of glue.

2 Press header molding into position over window. Adhesive will hold molding to wall. For additional security, carefully hammer a #8 finishing nail into center of each side of molding.

3 Cut two lengths of molding equal to measurement from bottom of header molding to top of windowsill. Apply wood adhesive to back of molding strips and press into place. Secure with #8 finishing nails.

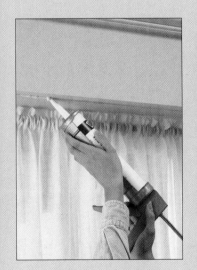

4 Use latex painter's caulk and caulk gun to conceal any gaps between window molding and walls. To conceal tops of finishing nails, cover them with wood putty and sand flat before painting.

5 When all molding is in position and glue and caulk are dry, apply one or two coats of latex paint to camouflage nail holes. Protect window and adjacent wall with pieces of plastic or newspaper.

HANDY HINTS

When you have finished caulking, remove the caulk tubes or cartridges from the gun. Place a large nail in the tip of the tube on the cartridge to prevent any remaining caulk from drying out.

Before attempting to glue any two surfaces, make sure both are clean and dry. Be sure to mark their placement first, since once two surfaces are glued together, they may be difficult to reposition.

TAKE NOTE

Wood adhesive is very flammable. Store it away from heat in a dry place. Work with adhesive in well-ventilated rooms.

DOLLAR SENSE

Plastic molding is relatively inexpensive and holds up well in high-traffic areas. This makes it particularly suitable for use in children's rooms. It is available unfinished or prefinished in several different colors.

Fabric-Covered Cornice Boards

Cornice boards add architectural interest to windows and doors.

You Will Need
- ❏ 1- by 4-inch pine board
- ❏ 1- by 12-inch pine board
- ❏ Fabric & quilt batting
- ❏ Eyelet picture hooks
- ❏ Wood glue
- ❏ Finishing nails
- ❏ Hammer, screwdriver & saw
- ❏ Staple gun & staples
- ❏ Yardstick, right-angle ruler & pencil

BEFORE YOU BEGIN

A cornice treatment will draw the eye upward no matter what style or color fabric you choose.

Measuring the Window

Measure the window dimensions accurately. Then follow these calculations to ensure a successful project.

The finished cornice board measures 12 inches wider and 4 inches deeper than window measurements. Measure window width from outside edge of molding. If window has an outside-mounted window treatment, measure the rod from end to end instead.

Measure window length from top of molding, or rod, to sill. The cornice depth should not exceed one-fifth the total length of the window.

Cutting and Marking Boards

From 12-inch board: Cut one face board 4 inches longer than window width.

From 4-inch board: Cut one mounting board 2½ inches longer than window width. Cut two legs, each 12 inches long.

Mark boards: Mark two parallel pencil lines 2 inches and 3 inches from top edge of face board; pencil these markings on front and back of board. Measure and mark center of face and mounting boards.

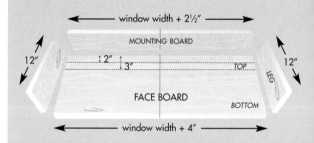

Cutting and Marking Fabrics

Batting: Cutting length = 2x depth of face board. Cutting width = width of face board + 4x width of leg.

Fabric: Cutting length = 2x depth of face board + 6 inches. Cutting width = width of face board + (4x width of leg) + 6 inches.

Mark fabric: To locate center, fold fabric and batting in half vertically. Mark fold at each long edge.

ASSEMBLING THE BOARD

HANDY HINTS

Most printed fabric must be mounted vertically to keep the motifs right side up. For wide windows, piece together several panels of fabric. Position the main motif in the center of the face board. For solids or when the print allows, position the fabric horizontally.

1 Apply wood glue to one long end of each leg. With edges even, place legs on underside of face board. Hold firmly in place for a few minutes to allow glue to set. Hammer at least three finishing nails through face board into center of legs to hold them securely in place.

2 Apply wood glue to one long end and two short ends of mounting board. Position it between pencil markings on face board. Using markings as a guide, hammer finishing nails through face board into mounting board. Also nail legs to mounting board.

3 Matching center markings, staple batting to assembly back at top edge of mounting board. Wrap batting smoothly around assembly front to lower half of back; staple to back. Wrap batting around legs; staple, covering all surfaces and trimming where necessary.

4 Fold under 1 inch on top edge of fabric. Staple to cornice assembly as done with batting in Step 3, keeping fabric taut. Trim where necessary to avoid bulk, turning under cut edges of fabric before stapling.

5 On remaining long edge, turn under enough fabric (1 to 2 inches) to align evenly with bottom edge of mounting board. Staple folded edge of fabric to assembly back along bottom edge of mounting board.

6 Measuring 4 inches from each side edge, attach two picture hooks to mounting board. For wide windows, attach several more hooks 12 to 18 inches apart. Mount to wall above window.

CAFE CURTAINS

Give a window luxuriously full gathers with double-rodded cafes.

YOU WILL NEED

❏ FABRIC
❏ CURTAIN RODS
❏ SEWING MACHINE
❏ IRON
❏ MEASURING TAPE
❏ THREAD
❏ FABRIC SHEARS
❏ PINS

BEFORE YOU BEGIN

Before buying curtain fabric, work out all the details for rod placement and fabric width for bunching.

Determine Measurements

Determine the length and width of the fabric needed.
• For the drop length, measure the distance between the rods and add ½ inch for drape.
• To that add three times the diameter of one curtain rod (enough for both) plus 2 inches to make a ½-inch double hem at top and bottom.

• Determine the width of the fabric needed.
• Measure the total length of the hung curtain rod or measure the width of the area to be covered. Double that measurement for heavy fabrics; triple it for light-weight ones.

Positioning Rods

Select rods and attach them to the window or position tension rods. Tension rods are best suited for double-rod curtains. They require no hardware and adjust easily if curtain is too short or too long.

Permanent Rod Measurements

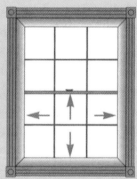

Tension Rod Measurements

Choosing Fabric

• The choice of fabric depends on available light and room decor. An obvious lead is to pick a prominent color from the surroundings.
• If the window faces north, use a light color, a loose weave or lace to let in a maximum of the outside light.
• For a window facing direct light, choose a fabric that will not fade easily.

SEWING CAFE CURTAINS

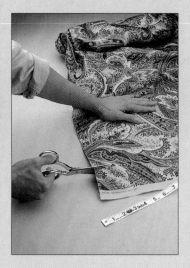

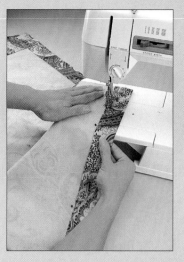

1 Cut the fabric according to the determined measurements. Make sure to cut at a right angle to the selvage so the grain of the fabric is straight and exactly vertical and horizontal.

2 To hem the side edges, turn under 1 inch and press, then turn 1 inch under again and press to create a double hem. A double hem adds strength to the curtain sides and creates a finished, professional look.

3 Pin the hems carefully and stitch very close to the first fold, now at the inside of the fabric. Remove the pins as you sew to avoid any puckering. Also, machine sewing over pins may break a needle.

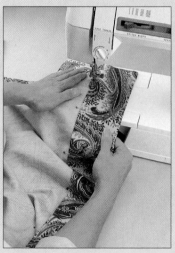

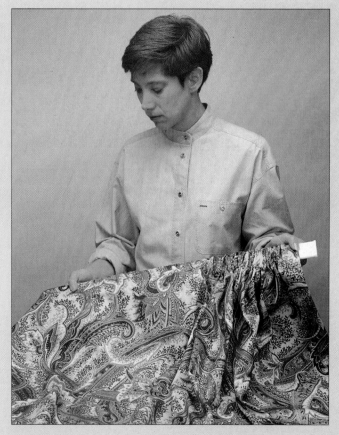

4 Along the top edge, turn under ½ inch twice and press in place. Then turn under 1½ times the diameter of the rod pocket, making sure it is even across the width of the curtain. Press again.

5 Pin down the fold for the rod pocket. Stitch close to the edge of the fold so there is room for the rod to slip through. Remove the pins as you sew. Repeat steps for the bottom rod.

6 Insert the curtain rod into the rod pocket, being careful not to catch the fabric. Hang the rod and adjust the fabric so that the gathers are evenly spaced.

SIMPLE POCKET-STYLE CURTAINS

Elegant and easy, these lovely curtains are a breeze to make.

BEFORE YOU BEGIN

To make pocket-style curtains, fold the top of the fabric over to form the rod pocket and heading. Fit the rod to the wall before working out fabric lengths.

Figuring Fabric Measurements

Decide on the length of the finished curtain (measure bottom of pole to hem). Add a double hem and turning allowance as follows:
• At the top, add the depth of the rod pocket (1½ x rod diameter) to heading depth. Double this figure and add ½ inch for hem.
• At the bottom of the curtain, add at least 2 inches for a double-turned hem.

Decide on the width of the curtain as follows:
• Multiply the length of the rod by 2 to 2½ for medium and heavy fabrics, 2½ to 3 for sheer fabrics.
• Add 3 inches for each side hem.

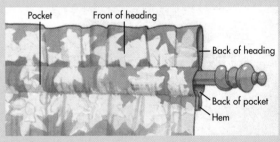

The top folds over, which is why the measurement is doubled.

Matching Patterns

Check how many pattern repeats are required down each curtain. It may be necessary to buy extra fabric to get patterns to match on both curtains (below). If joining widths, make sure that the patterns also match at these seams.

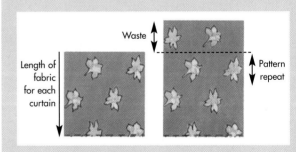

SEWING POCKET-STYLE CURTAINS

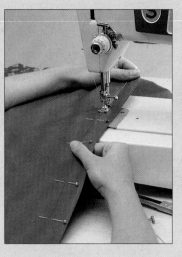

1 Cut fabric lengths. Join panels, if necessary, to get desired fullness. To join widths, lay selvages right sides together. Press top edge back and match pattern (if any) across the seam. Pin to hold.

2 Unfold the selvage and repin carefully along the fold line. Check the pattern match on the right side. Repin again, placing pins at right angles to fold line. Stitch along fold line. Trim panel to length.

3 Sew side hems next. Press a double fold to the wrong side of fabric and pin. Machine stitch close to the first fold or slipstitch by hand if you do not want the stitching to show on the right side.

HANDY HINTS

Unlined curtains in south-facing windows may fade quickly in the sun. So avoid using expensive fabrics or consider lining them.

For short-length curtains, avoid deep pattern repeats —matching the pattern will waste material.

DOLLAR SENSE

For a pair of old curtains that are beginning to look worn, simply cut off the curtain heading and hems and use panels to create a smaller, pocket-style curtain.

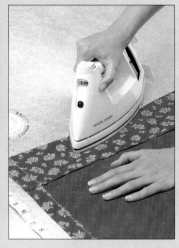

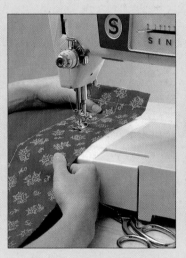

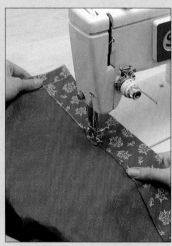

4 Press ½ inch of fabric along the upper edge of panel to the wrong side. Fold pressed edge down to form the casing (depth equal to heading + rod pocket). Press and pin in place, then stitch close to turned edge.

5 To make the rod pocket, form a parallel line of stitching at a distance equal to 1½ times rod diameter from the last line of stitching. Stick tape to the machine as a guide to keep stitching straight.

6 Form a simple double hem by folding the lower curtain edge under twice. Press hem, pin, and then stitch close to the first fold, or slipstitch by hand for an invisible hem on the right side.

PAINTED SHADES WITH AN EDGE

Dress up plastic shades with a unique design in just a few hours.

YOU WILL NEED

- ❏ PLASTIC ROLLER SHADE
- ❏ ARTIST'S ACRYLIC PAINTS
- ❏ ½-INCH ROUND BRUSH
- ❏ PAINTER'S MASKING TAPE
- ❏ COLORED PENCILS
- ❏ GUM ERASER
- ❏ SCISSORS
- ❏ SCRAP PAPER
- ❏ SPONGE
- ❏ PAINT TRAY

BEFORE YOU BEGIN

Paint simple motifs—inspired by wallpaper, fabric or a children's book—on a ready-made plastic shade.

Measuring for Shade Size

To determine the size of the shade, measure the interior length and width of the window frame in two spots. Select the shortest.
- Shades can be cut to fit in most stores where they are sold.
- The standard shade is usually plastic with a low-sheen surface.
- Revive old paper shades by painting with gesso on both sides. Then paint with white or cream artist's acrylic paint. Gesso and

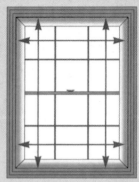

acrylic paint are available in art supply stores.

Planning and Practice

On paper, roughly sketch the placement of the stripes, swirls and equal signs. Use colored pencils to plan a balanced distribution of the swirls and equal signs. Try several versions before deciding on the final design.

Practice painting swirls and equal signs on a large scrap of paper. Begin painting swirls at the center. The paint will be heavier at the start of the stroke, lighter at the end. Touch up if necessary.

PAINTING THE SHADE

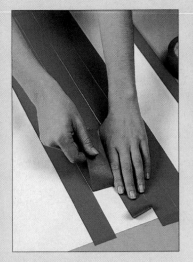

1 Lay the shade out flat. Stick a strip of painter's masking tape along the bottom edge following the stitching. Apply eight more strips of tape side by side, edges even. Peel off 2nd, 3rd, 6th and 7th strips.

2 Pour paint for the stripes into a small paint tray. Dip the sponge in paint and dab on scrap paper to remove excess. Lightly sponge the stripes formed by the tape. Let paint dry before removing the tape.

3 Lightly pencil in the swirls and equal signs following the plan. Erase any mistakes with a gum eraser. Position the bottom edges of the lowest swirls and equal signs about 2 inches above the top stripe.

HANDY HINTS

To integrate the shade into the design of the room, pick up the color or colors from the window frame, the wall paint or the wallpaper.

For a finishing touch, select something of interest to hang on the shade pull, such as a small toy, wooden honey dip, crystal bead or silk tassel.

QUICK FIX

Keep a damp rag handy to wipe spills or unwanted strokes. Freshly painted acrylic paint comes off easily with soap and water.

4 Working with one color at a time, put just enough paint on the brush so that it does not drip. Paint each swirl and equal sign. Go over swirls again, if necessary, to ensure a good cover of paint.

5 Wash the brush well between colors. When finished, look over the painted shade carefully for any areas that need touching up. When the paint has completely dried, gently erase any pencil marks that are still visible with a gum eraser.

Clever Ways to Hang Curtains

A fancy rod and pretty cording make a simple sheer really special.

36

YOU WILL NEED
- ❏ Sheer fabric
- ❏ Cording
- ❏ Sewing machine
- ❏ Pins & thread
- ❏ Measuring tape
- ❏ Grommet kit
- ❏ Hammer
- ❏ Buckram
- ❏ Iron

BEFORE YOU BEGIN

To make grommeted curtains, attach grommet hardware at regular intervals across the curtain heading. Use a stiff interfacing to support sheer fabrics.

Figuring Fabric Measurements

Determine the length of the curtain by measuring from the top of the window molding to the upper edge of the sill. See diagram below.
• At the top, add 3½ inches for the heading which creates the buckram casing.
• At the bottom, add 2½ inches for the hem.

• The curtain width should be 1½ times the width of the window.
• Add 1 inch to each side for a ½-inch hem.
• The buckram for the heading should be 3 inches wide by 1½ times the width of the window.

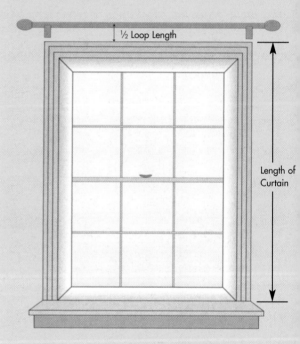

½ Loop Length

Length of Curtain

Placing Grommets

Determine how many grommets are desired. One grommet should be at each side, usually about ½ inch from the edge. The rest of the grommets should be evenly spaced along the top. An odd number of grommets usually creates a more pleasing arrangement.

MAKING CURTAINS WITH GROMMET HOLES

1 Cut panels to desired width. Press under ½ inch on each side of panel. Press under 1½ inches again. Open out folds at bottom. Press bottom edge under ½ inch Press under 2 inches again and pin in place. Stitch along inner fold of hem.

2 At top edge, press under 1 inch. Press under 3 inches again. Open folds; place length of buckram under short fold, between curtain and overlap. Pin overlap in place, catching overlap, buckram and curtain.

3 Stitch through buckram and curtain header close to each folded edge, catching fabric overlap at top edge. Pin folded side edges in place; stitch side seams close to inside folded edges; secure at edges.

4 Using a measuring tape and chalk, mark grommet positions across curtain heading as discussed in Before You Begin. Make marks in center of header fabric equidistant from other grommets.

5 Center grommets vertically in heading, making sure the edges of the side grommets are touching the marks and the others are centered on their marks. Attach according to manufacturer's instructions.

6 Knot one end of cord. Thread cord through grommets from back to front. Slide rod through loops and hang above window. Adjust cord loops to desired length. Tie ends neatly and cut off excess.

PAINT EFFECTS ON GLASS

Fun, painted designs add a lighthearted touch of color to a window.

BEFORE YOU BEGIN

Pictures from a favorite book—or the outlines from a coloring book—come to life when transferred to the panes of glass in a child's room.

Preparing the Pattern

Painting on glass adds color to the window and the entire room, entertaining the eye while adding a unique decoration.

The application isn't permanent; it will need touch-ups eventually.

Once the design is chosen, size it to fit the panes of glass. Enlarge or reduce an existing design on a photocopier or draw freehand onto plain paper.

Tape the pattern behind the glass and trace the outline on the front.

Or add a chalk coating to the back of the design paper, place the paper on the front of the glass and transfer the design.

Rub chalk over entire back of pattern paper (below left). Hold pattern on window with masking tape. Using a ball point pen or rounded surface, trace the design outlines.

Lift up one pattern edge to be sure chalk lines have transferred onto window (below right). Fill in any missing areas. When complete, remove pattern and use as a color guide.

Tools and Paint

The right tools and paint make this job easy.
• Use a marking pen that will write on any surface.
• Use small artist's brushes with tips sized for the area you need to cover.

• Use artist's acrylics or oil-based paints. Acrylics are easier to work with. If using oil paint, do not dip brush in water.

PAINTING ON GLASS

1 Tape the full-sized pattern to the back of the window with the right side facing inside the window. Following the lines of the design, use a black marker to trace the design onto the window. Remove design.

2 Put a small amount of paint on a palette. Dip the brush in water before dipping into paint. Work with one color at a time, filling in all areas. Apply several coats of paint to ensure an even application.

3 When the first color is dry, apply the second color of paint. Work from the top to the bottom of the window pane to avoid rubbing it against wet paint. Continue adding colors until the picture is complete.

HANDY HINTS

Keep a small cup of water nearby to dip brush occasionally while painting. If the acrylic paint gets too thick, a little water will thin it. If using oil-based paint, keep a cup of mineral spirits handy for thinning the paint.

TAKE NOTE

Put window cleaner on a cloth to clean around the painted area. Do not spray cleaner on the window directly or the acrylic paint will run. Use a dry cloth on painted areas.

4 Paint the final outline of the design in black using a thin paintbrush or the black marker that was used to trace the design. Store the leftover paints in case touch-ups are needed later on. Do not wash the painted areas.

Window Shelf Display

Use this simple shelf to highlight a view and create a pretty display.

You Will Need

- ❑ Five-quarter board
- ❑ Shelf brackets
- ❑ 1½ inch finishing nails
- ❑ Mounting hardware
- ❑ Wood glue & putty
- ❑ Sandpaper & tack cloth
- ❑ Wood stain & brush
- ❑ Hammer & nail punch
- ❑ Straightedge & pencil

BEFORE YOU BEGIN

For a perfect fit, take measurements before shopping for wood. The final dimensions of the shelf will be determined by the size of the window and the width of the bracket you choose.

Preparing the Wood

- The shelf should extend 1 inch beyond each bracket. Each bracket should be set 1½ inches from the outer edge of the window frame.
- Length of shelf = width of window + width of both brackets + 2 inches + 3 inches.
- Mark shelf dimensions on board in pencil. Cut to size.
- Sand all edges of brackets and board with medium sandpaper, then again with fine paper. Wipe shelf with lint-free cloth to remove all traces of dust.

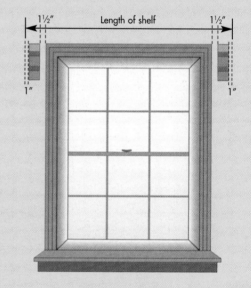

Final Touches

- Apply a coat of polyurethane to seal the finished shelf.
- Screw S-hooks into the underside of the shelf and use them to hang wicker baskets and bunches of dried flowers.
- To attach the brackets to the wall, insert two screws into the wall and hook the metal plate in the brackets over the top. Check manufacturer's instructions for details.

A wide variety of brackets—from very plain to extremely ornate—is available from lumberyards to suit almost any style of window shelf.

ASSEMBLING THE SHELF

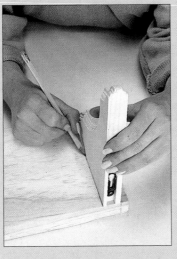

HANDY HINTS

To hold the shelf securely in place, hammer long nails through the top of the shelf down into the window molding.

1 Use a straightedge and pencil to measure and mark a line on the top and bottom sides of the shelf, ½ inch from each short end.

2 Hold the bracket in position along the inside of the marked line. Mark the thickness of the bracket by lightly drawing a pencil line on the top and bottom of the shelf, along the inside of the bracket. Repeat at the other end.

3 On the top of the shelf, evenly space three nails in the middle of the parallel pencil lines at one end. Hammer in the nails until they begin to appear on the underside of the shelf. Repeat with three nails at the other end of the shelf.

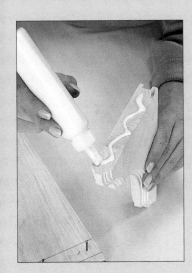

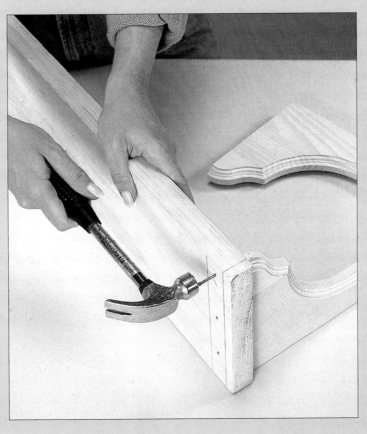

4 Apply wood glue to the top of one bracket. Position the bracket between the parallel lines on the underside of one end of the shelf; hold in place for a few seconds. Repeat at the other end of the shelf. Allow glue to dry completely.

5 Hammer the nails through the shelf and bracket at both ends. Using a nail punch, countersink the nails below the surface of the wood. Erase pencil lines. Apply wood putty to hide the nail holes; sand smooth. Stain all surfaces of the shelf and brackets.

FROSTED DESIGNS ON GLASS

Give plain glass panes a facelift with this easy etching technique.

YOU WILL NEED

- ❏ GLASS ETCHING CREAM
- ❏ FOAM BRUSH
- ❏ CLEAR SELF-ADHESIVE COVERING
- ❏ CRAFT KNIFE
- ❏ STENCIL
- ❏ PENCIL
- ❏ PLAIN PAPER
- ❏ PAINTER'S MASKING TAPE
- ❏ CLEAN SPONGE

BEFORE YOU BEGIN

Etching is a very easy technique to master. Before beginning, make sure the glass has been properly prepared and the design has been carefully planned.

Preparing the Glass

Follow these simple directions to prepare the glass for etching:
- Clean and dry the glass with a lint-free cloth.
- Mask the wood to protect it from the etching cream and rinse water.
- If the glass cannot be laid flat for etching, tape a plastic drop cloth below the area to be etched. Place the other end of the drop cloth into a bucket to catch the rinse water as it flows off.

Preparing the Design

Enlarge the stencil below to the desired size on a photocopier, trace it onto thin cardboard and cut it out with a sharp craft knife. Remember to add registration marks so that each part of the stenciled design lines up.

Cut a piece of paper to the exact shape and size of the glass. Use the stencil to draw the design in the desired position on the paper.

When stenciling a border, keep the design straight by lining it up with a pencil line drawn on the paper.

ETCHING THE GLASS

HANDY HINTS

If clear self-adhesive covering is not available, use carbon paper to trace the design onto a piece of opaque self-adhesive covering instead.

Create frosted designs on window panes to the outside, too. This technique doesn't need to be restricted to the glass cupboard doors shown here.

1 Remove the doors from the cabinet. Place the paper with the traced design facedown on the inside of the glass, so that the design shows through to the right side. Fix in place with masking tape.

2 Trace the shape and size of the glass onto self-adhesive covering. Using scissors, cut the self-adhesive covering to size. Carefully peel off the backing and stick the covering onto the front of the glass.

3 Using a sharp craft knife, follow the traced lines to cut out the design from the self-adhesive covering. Take care when cutting around corners to ensure that the lines are smooth, with no jagged edges.

4 Wearing rubber gloves, use a foam brush to apply glass etching cream to the areas that have been cut away from the self-adhesive covering. Make sure the whole design area is well covered with the cream.

5 Leave the etching cream on the glass for the length of time recommended by the manufacturer. When the time has elapsed, carefully peel off the self-adhesive covering to reveal the etched design.

6 Wipe down the etched side of the glass thoroughly with a sponge and clean water. Remove the traced design from the back of the glass. Repeat the etching process with the second cabinet door. When the designs are complete, rehang the doors on the cabinet.

SECOND-CHANCE
FURNITURE

Furniture seldom breaks outright. It just gets sort of tired looking, or falls out of favor with your tastes and the times. And sometimes a person just looks at a table, chair, headboard, dresser, cabinet, drawer or other item, and wants something new. But why throw out a perfectly good piece of furniture when you can give it a quick, easy and beautiful makeover? Whether you use fabric, paint, stain, stencils or something else, it's time to give furniture a second chance. We're betting there's a lot of life left in it!

THE LOOK OF INLAID WOOD

Embellish wooden furniture with a twist on the art of marquetry.

YOU WILL NEED

- ❑ GEL WOOD STAINS
- ❑ MASKING TAPE
- ❑ FOAM BRUSHES
- ❑ SOFT, CLEAN RAGS
- ❑ TRACING PAPER
- ❑ T SQUARE
- ❑ METAL RULER & PENCIL
- ❑ GRAPHITE PAPER
- ❑ ACETATE SHEETS
- ❑ CRAFT KNIFE
- ❑ POLYURETHANE

BEFORE YOU BEGIN

For authentic-looking inlaid wood patterns, go to the source for inspiration; adapt actual inlaid designs from woodworking pieces you admire.

Creating a Pattern

The most important step in imitating the look of inlaid furniture is to create a pattern that is easy to reproduce using painter's masking tape.

• Draw your checkerboard design and border on a piece of tracing paper using a T square and ruler to ensure straight lines. To avoid intricate cutting, consider the widths of masking tape available and plan the design accordingly. Masking tape is available in widths ranging from ¼ inch to 3 inches. Make the sides of the squares equal to the width of the tape.

• Use colored pencils on the tracing paper pattern to indicate what colors should be used in the final design.

• When you have finalized a full-sized pattern (below), lay clear acetate over the tracing paper. With a ruler, carefully copy the design onto the acetate.

Painting Preparation

To begin, prepare the surface for painting. Wipe clean with a soft rag. Sand with a fine-grade sandpaper. Wipe away the dust. Repeat process, if necessary.

When applying masking tape, be sure to press the edges flat with your finger to prevent the stain from seeping under.

Use only gel stains—they are easier to control since regular stains will seep more easily under the masking tape. Gel stains are available in a variety of colors including metallics and decorator colors, as well as wood tones. They are easily found at hardware and craft stores.

STAINING AN INLAID PATTERN

1 Lay a piece of graphite paper on wood surface; then lay acetate design on top. Using a pencil and metal ruler, carefully trace pattern lines so they transfer graphite onto wood surface.

2 Using correct width of masking tape for each part of design, place tape horizontally over surface. Press tape flat along the edges to seal. Using a craft knife, lightly cut along vertical design lines.

3 Choose first color of gel you wish to apply. Referring to colored pattern, remove tape squares from areas to be stained with first gel; place on acetate pattern. Press tape flat along edges to prevent seepage.

HANDY HINTS

When removing tape from the wood surface, be sure to cut only as far as the design edge, or the stain may bleed into another design area.

TAKE NOTE

This masking tape method makes the project easier and faster. However, the tape may not adhere when reapplied over the stained area if conditions are humid or hot.

4 Using a foam brush, lightly paint exposed squares with gel. Wipe excess stain from surface with a soft, clean rag; reapply stain if a darker color is desired. When stain is dry, replace tape squares that were set aside onto stained squares. Then, remove tape from unstained squares. Following staining process above, paint newly exposed squares to complete checkerboard design.

5 Once center design is completed and dry, remove tape squares. For a border, apply a narrower tape around edges of the design and another piece parallel to first, about 1 inch from surface's edge. Stain between tapes; allow to dry and remove tape. Apply a protective coating of polyurethane finish to the surface. Paint at least three coats, lightly sanding and wiping surface clean between coats.

CRACKLE FINISH

Oil and water form an intriguing crazed finish for wood.

YOU WILL NEED

❑ WOOD FURNITURE
❑ LATEX SEMIGLOSS PAINT
❑ PAINTBRUSHES
❑ CRACKLE GLAZE OR GUM ARABIC
❑ DISH DETERGENT
❑ POLYURETHANE

BEFORE YOU BEGIN

In crackle glazing, the degree of contrast or coordination of the topcoat and base coat yields results that run from subtle to sensational.

Crackle Glaze Basics

For a dramatic effect, use two strongly contrasting paint colors (left top and left middle). For a more subtle, traditional finished effect, use two paint colors that are more closely related (left bottom).

The direction in which the crackle glaze is brushed on determines the crack formation.

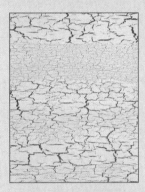

Brushing every which way yields the most random, all-over crackle pattern, while straight strokes will produce a fairly uniform effect.

Because crackle glaze tends to fall off if worked vertically, use horizontal brush strokes as much as possible.

For finer crackling, apply a thin coat of paint. For more pronounced crackling, brush on a generous top coat.

Dry with a hair dryer for bolder crackling effects.

Do not use a crackle paint effect on items that will need washing.

Preparation

• If you will be applying a crackle finish to an old piece of furniture, it is important that you create a surface the paint and glaze will adhere to by sanding it lightly before you begin painting.

• If the furniture is new, sand it lightly, brush on a coat of wood primer, let it dry thoroughly and then sand it lightly once again before starting to paint.

CRACKLE GLAZING ON FURNITURE

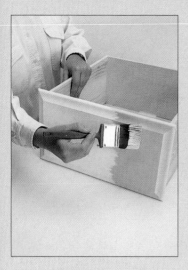

1 Start the project by painting the bureau drawers. Brush a base coat of latex semigloss paint in the color of your choice onto the drawer. This will be the color of the cracks. Let the paint dry for 24 hours.

2 Stir a drop or two of dish detergent into the crackle glaze to keep it from separating as it is painted on. Brush a coat of crackle glaze or gum arabic onto the bureau. Leave to dry for several hours.

3 Working quickly, use a roller or brush to apply a top coat of paint onto the drawer. Overlap the strips of paint but do not go over an area a second time as the crackle is very volatile and will slide off until it is dry.

HANDY HINTS

Crackle glaze, available at specialty paint stores and art supply shops, is basically a sticky liquid that interferes with the way paint adheres to the surface, resulting in a cracked surface.

When working with a dresser or desk, remove the drawers and knobs and refinish them separately.

DOLLAR SENSE

Gum arabic and crackle glaze are about the same price and can be used interchangeably for this project.

4 After the crackle finish has had a chance to dry for about 24 hours, brush two coats of polyurethane onto the bureau. This will prevent the crackle from flaking off when touched. Repeat Steps 1-4 for the rest of the bureau.

SIMPLE UPHOLSTERED HEADBOARDS

Add definition to the head of the bed with a colorful headboard.

BEFORE YOU BEGIN

To determine the best size and placement for a headboard, tape a paper rectangle on the wall. Adjust the height and width until you are satisfied.

Cutting the Fabric and Foam

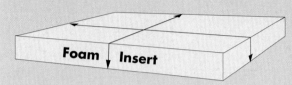

For best results, it is important to accurately measure and cut the fabric and foam.
• Using paper shape as a guide for size, purchase 3-inch-thick foam. If possible, have the foam cut to size professionally.
• To cut the foam yourself, use a marker to draw the shape on the foam. Cut on the lines with a craft knife or an electric knife.
• To determine headboard width, add the width and the depth of the foam plus 1 inch for seam allowances. Repeat for the height of the foam.
• Cut two pieces of fabric following the grainline of the bed sheet. If you're using decorator fabric, piecing may be necessary to equal the width of the headboard. Add pieces of equal width to the sides of a center panel rather than stitching a seam down the middle.

Headboard Hints

The correct position of the headboard is crucial to its appearance. Use a paper

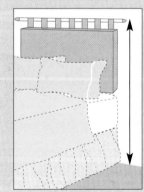

rectangle to determine where it looks best; mark the corners. Always center the headboard over the bed and make sure that its bottom edge is even with the bed or up to 3 inches higher.

When hanging the curtain rod, include additional length for the ribbon ties. It might be helpful to tie the ribbons to the rod to determine the required hanging space between rod and headboard.

MAKING THE HEADBOARD

1 Cut two pieces of fabric (Before You Begin). Cut ribbon into eight 18-inch lengths. Fold ribbons in half; pin them to right side of fabric at upper edge, with ribbons' folded edges against fabric's raw edge.

2 With right sides facing and raw edges aligned, stitch two pieces of headboard fabric together, catching folded edge of ribbons in top seam and leaving a wide opening along the bottom edge.

3 Press top seam open so that each end forms a point. Using a ruler and pencil, draw a 3-inch line across point, perpendicular to seam. Stitch over pencil mark. Repeat for remaining three corners.

4 Trim points near stitching lines leaving ½-inch seam allowances. Turn headboard cover right side out and press seams flat. Carefully insert foam headboard piece into fabric cover, positioning cover so that corners of foam fit snugly into corners of fabric.

5 Smooth fabric casing over bottom of foam. Turn raw edges to inside along seamline; pin edges together. Slipstitch opening closed. Tie ribbons around curtain rod at desired length and hang headboard over bed. Once in place, ribbons may need adjusting to make headboard hang straight. Remove as needed for laundering. Consider making additional covers to match other sheet sets for bed.

DECORATIVE TABLETOP TILES

Tile your tabletop for an attractive, durable and heat-resistant finish.

YOU WILL NEED

- ❏ TILE
- ❏ TILE ADHESIVE
- ❏ GROUT
- ❏ NOTCHED ADHESIVE TROWEL
- ❏ HAMMER & 1-INCH HEADLESS BRADS
- ❏ SPONGES
- ❏ ½-INCH-WIDE LATTICE
- ❏ SANDPAPER
- ❏ SAW

BEFORE YOU BEGIN

Search the attic, tag sales or consignment shops for a suitable table to renovate with tiles.

Preparing the Table for Tiling

Use a square or rectangular table with sturdy legs that can support the weight of the tiles. Refinish the sides and legs of the table as desired. If painting, apply paint, let dry, and seal with a polyurethane finish.

• Clean the tabletop to remove sawdust and grime. Roughen the surface with sandpaper.

• Using a pencil and ruler, draw a grid in 2-inch squares on the tabletop as a guide for tile placement.

• Determine the width of the lattice trim to be attached to the sides of the tabletop. Measure the depth of the tabletop, add the thickness of the tiles to be used plus at least ⅛ inch for tile adhesive.

Choosing Tiles

Measure the tabletop, including the size of the border tiles and determine the best size of tile to use. Try to avoid choosing tiles that require cutting to size.

Shop around for different types of tile (right). Some border tiles are bullnosed, or rounded, on one side for a finished edge. Square tiles are available in 2-, 4-, 6- and 8-inch squares and often have built-in spacers. Specialty tiles (below) are available in many lengths and widths.

TILING A TABLETOP

HANDY HINTS

Once the tile and grout have set, apply a grout sealer over the grout to provide a stain-resistant barrier.

1 Cut two pieces of lattice the same length as the short side of the tabletop, and two pieces the length of the long side plus two times the thickness of the lattice. Apply two coats of paint to the wood; let dry.

2 With bottom edges aligned, the lattice trim should be higher than the tabletop (Before You Begin); nail the wood pieces around all sides of the tabletop. Fill nail holes with putty, smooth with sandpaper, and paint.

3 Working on a clean surface, apply a thick coat of tile adhesive, at least $\frac{1}{8}$ inch, at the edge of the tabletop so that the tiles will be level with edge of the border. Cover only as much area as you can work on before it dries.

4 Beginning in one corner of the table, apply border tiles. Butt the tiles against the wood frame. Avoid moving them once they are positioned. Continue around the table's edges until all border tiles are applied.

5 Starting from a corner and working out in small sections, apply 4-inch tiles to the tabletop. Set the tiles next to each other, leaving about $\frac{1}{8}$ inch between them. Align with border tiles for an even finish.

6 Once the tiles have set, use a sponge to spread grout between them. Apply a heavy coat of grout to ensure that all spaces are filled. Wipe off excess grout with clean water and sponges until all the tiles are clean. When the grout dries, use a glass cleaner and soft cloth to wipe away film.

CHARMING PUNCHED TIN CABINETS

The traditional decorating technique of punching tin is easy and effective.

BEFORE YOU BEGIN

Geometric shapes, natural motifs and religious symbols are traditional patterns for punched tin.

Creating a Template

When choosing a design, keep in mind that simple shapes are often more effective because they are easier to distinguish.
• Transfer the rooster template (below) to a piece of paper and enlarge it to fit within the center dimensions of the tin panel.

• Transfer and enlarge the geometric design (below left) to fit around the panel's edges for a border.
• Using a scrap of tin, test a variety of tools—like awls, chisels, nails and screwdrivers—to create different punched shapes.

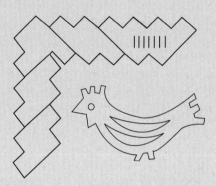

Tips for Working with Tin

Tin sheets suitable for punching are available in craft stores. These small sheets are usually craft-grade tin and not as thick as utility-grade tin.

Larger pieces of tin can be purchased at home supply or hardware centers. Use tin snips to cut tin to size, or have the sheet cut professionally at a hardware supply or welding shop.

For an exact fit, remove the wood panel from the cabinet door and use it as a pattern for cutting tin.

Before punching, always lay tin on a flat, wooden work surface. Keep in mind that punching the tin will mar the surface underneath.

Wear heavy utility gloves when handling tin, since the edges can be sharp. If desired, have the sides of the tin crimped to eliminate the sharp edges.

Awls and screwdrivers make round holes in tin, while chisels create slashes. The larger the diameter of the tool tip, the larger the punched hole will be. Keep holes and slashes from overlapping on the tin so that the punched pattern remains intact.

PUNCHING TIN PANELS

HANDY HINTS

Keep tin from rusting by rubbing it with a soft cloth dampened with machine oil. Rub both sides until the oil has soaked into the tin.

For a weathered look, cover the tin with a specialty paint finish. A glazed finish antiques the tin, while a verdigris finish adds a soft patina to its surface.

QUICK FIX

To hide the edges of the tin, cut pieces of wood trim to fit around the panel's recess and hammer in place with headless brads.

1 Cover all the edges of tin with masking tape. If desired, add another layer of tape as protection from the tin's sharp edges. Using a pencil and ruler, lightly mark the center of the tin for pattern placement.

2 Using a ruler, mark a border that is equal to or wider than the recess on the door. Using the center mark and border as a guide, center the template (Before You Begin) on the tin and tape it in place.

3 Working from the center outward on a wood surface, begin punching holes by gently tapping the top of the punching tool with a hammer on the design. Vary tools (Before You Begin) for the desired shape.

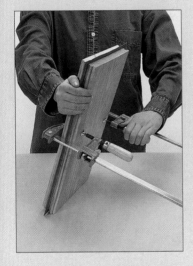

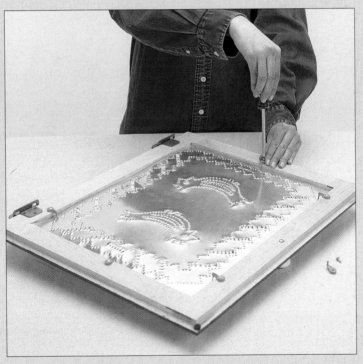

4 When the punched design is complete, flatten the dents by sandwiching the tin between two pieces of wood the same size. Fasten C clamps around the pieces of wood and leave it in place for 24 hours; remove.

5 With the front facing down, reposition the tin in the recess of the door. Secure the door with the original hardware, screwing the brackets through the tin, if necessary. Wipe the punched design clean with a damp cloth.

CLEVER BATHTUB MAKEOVERS

Make a splash in your bath with these clever bathtub makeovers.

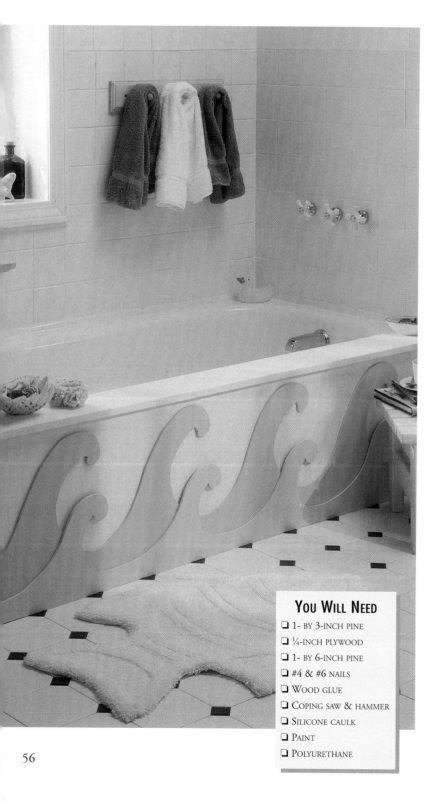

BEFORE YOU BEGIN

Use your imagination when creating decorative wooden cutout shapes for the front of the bathtub.

Cutting the Frame and Panels

Before cutting, measure the width and height of the front of your bathtub.

• For the frame, use 1- by 3-inch pine. Cut two pieces equal to the width. Cut six pieces for the height, subtracting the width of the top and bottom pieces from the height measurement.

• From the plywood, cut one front and two side panels following the dimensions of the frame.

• Cut the top from 1- by 6-inch pine the length of the frame plus 2 inches.

Making Decorative Cutouts

For the height of the large wave, subtract 2 inches from the frame height. For the width, divide the frame by five. Repeat for the small wave, making its height half the tub height. Transfer the pattern to plywood and cut.

Sand and prime the waves; paint each a shade of blue.

Waterproofing the Panel

When you paint the front panel, add a mildew-resistant compound to the paint to retard the mildewing process.

To nail the frame together, use a high quality nail that won't rust when exposed to water and high humidity.

Paint and prime the front panel before securing it to the bathtub. Once in place, waterproof the panel's joints and seams by caulking them with silicone.

Available in clear or colors to match the porcelain, the silicone forms a protective barrier, keeping water from leaking between the tub and wooden frame.

BUILDING A DECORATIVE FRAME

1 Using a hammer and #4 nails, nail the frame together at the corners so the long top and bottom pieces of wood overlap the edges of the side pieces.

2 Position two short pieces of wood inside the frame and nail in place. Add extra braces by nailing a short piece to the ends of the frame at a 90° angle.

3 Center the frame against the front of the tub so the braces at the end are parallel to the wall. Using a hammer and #6 nails, nail the braces to the wall.

HANDY HINTS

If the wall is tiled around your tub, use a masonry bit to drill holes into the tile. Insert plastic anchors into the tile, then secure the frame by screwing through the wood and into the tile on the wall.

4 Apply wood glue along front edges of the frame. Position front panel over the frame, press into glue, then nail in place. Repeat for the two side panels.

5 Using a coping saw, cut a notch from each side of the top panel so the panel overlaps the edge of the tub and lies flat against the top of the frame.

6 Apply silicone to the edge of the tub and the top of the frame, then press the top panel in place. Using #6 nails, nail the top panel to the frame.

DOLLAR SENSE

Covering a bathtub with a wooden panel is an inexpensive way to disguise porcelain that has been damaged.

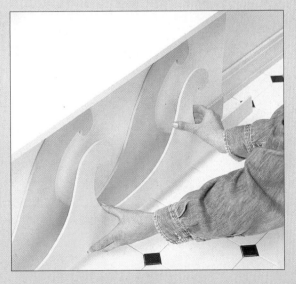

7 Apply wood glue to the back of the two baseboard pieces and glue to the side panels. Using #4 nails, nail the baseboard pieces to the panels.

8 Apply wood glue to the back of the large wave. Center the wave on the front panel, aligning the side edges. Using #4 nails, nail the wave in place. Next, glue and nail small wave over large wave, aligning side edges. Putty nail holes and touch up paint. Coat the panel with polyurethane.

EASY CUSHIONED FOOTSTOOL

Topped with fabric, this simple-to-make cushioned box becomes an elegant ottoman.

YOU WILL NEED

- ❏ 1- BY 4-INCH, 1- BY 6-INCH BOARDS & MOLDING
- ❏ WOODEN BALL FEET
- ❏ FABRIC, TRIM & BATTING
- ❏ 1½-INCH FINISHING NAILS
- ❏ GOLD PAINT & BRUSH
- ❏ FOAM RUBBER
- ❏ SCREWDRIVER & SCREWS
- ❏ WOOD GLUE & PUTTY
- ❏ STAPLE GUN & HAMMER
- ❏ GLUE GUN & GLUE STICKS
- ❏ RAZOR KNIFE

BEFORE YOU BEGIN

To simplify construction, ask the lumberyard to cut your boards to size.

Cut Sizes

The following is a list of sizes for the wood needed to construct the footstool.

For the top piece:
- two 18-inch pieces of 1- by 4-inch boards, one 18-inch piece of 1- by 6-inch.

For the bottom piece:
- two 18-inch pieces of 1- by 4-inch,
- one 18-inch piece of 1- by 6-inch.

For the side pieces:
- two 16½-inch pieces of 1- by 6-inch.

For the end piece:
- two 12½-inch pieces of 1- by 6-inch.

For the molding:
- two 2-foot pieces, two 18-inch pieces.

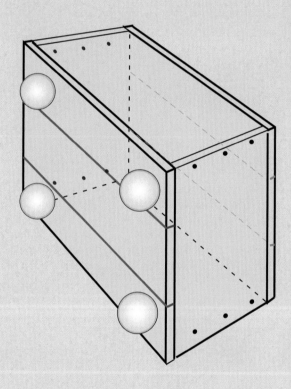

To determine dimensions for the upholstery fabric, first assemble the basic box (above). Measure from the top of the molding on one side, over the foam rubber, to the top of the molding on the other side. Repeat for the short sides, adding 2 inches to the measurements in each direction.

MAKING A CUSHIONED FOOTSTOOL

1 Glue and screw sides to ends, with ends overlapping the sides. Screw on the bottom pieces, with the wider board in the center. Glue and screw on the feet. Screw on top pieces.

2 Cut molding with a miter box to fit around the edges. Glue, aligning the bottom of the molding with the bottom of the box. Secure with 1½-inch finishing nails and patch with wood putty.

3 Brush a few coats of gold paint onto the molding and feet and let dry. While the paint dries, cut foam to fit the box top, beveling the top edges. An electric carving knife works well.

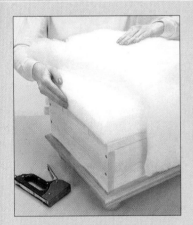

6 Put a staple into the fabric just above the molding on one long side. Pull the fabric to the left and continue stapling, stopping 3 inches from the corner. Continue to the right of center. Pull fabric taut over the foam.

4 Position the foam on the box. Cover with a piece of 10 ounce batting that is large enough to cover the top and reach the molding on each side.

5 Staple the batting just above the molding, pulling taut to secure opposite sides. Trim excess batting from the corners at the short sides. Fold excess from the long sides around corners and staple.

8 Trim excess fabric and batting below the staples and just above the molding with a razor knife. Cover the staples with decorative trim and secure with a glue gun. Hold the trim in place with pins until the glue has dried.

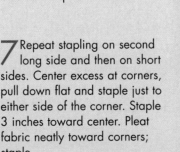

7 Repeat stapling on second long side and then on short sides. Center excess at corners, pull down flat and staple just to either side of the corner. Staple 3 inches toward center. Pleat fabric neatly toward corners; staple.

UPHOLSTERY TACK ACCENTS

Use upholstery tacks to add a unique touch to ordinary furniture.

BEFORE YOU BEGIN

Decorative upholstery tacks—with their large, domed heads and wide assortment of styles and colors—make wonderfully inexpensive and interesting decorating tools.

Decorating with Tacks

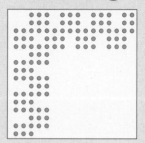

As an alternative to using chalk lines, make four same-size copies of the template (left). Tape the copies together to form the complete design. Make as many copies of the design as will appear on the piece of furniture.

There are many styles of upholstery tacks (right). Most have about ½-inch-diameter heads and come in several finishes, including brass, gold, silver and antiqued with plain or patterned heads.

Before hammering any tacks into furniture it is important to plan their placement on paper. This eliminates the possibility of an unbalanced design or unwanted tack holes.

Tape the paper template to the furniture surface. Apply the tacks directly onto the furniture through the template, taking care not to hammer the tacks all the way down. Once all the tacks are in place, remove the template by tearing it out from under the tacks. To finish, carefully hammer the tacks the remainder of the way down.

Setting Tacks

Most tacks are set with the gentle tap of a hammer.
• Cover delicate or etched tacks with a soft cloth to protect the heads from hammer marks or dents.
• If the wood is soft, the tacks might only need the push of a thumb to penetrate the surface.

• Use a thimble to protect your thumb when setting large quantities of tacks.
• An upholstery tack hammer is smaller than a standard hammer and is magnetized at one end.

DECORATING WITH TACKS

1 Mix equal parts paint and glaze. Paint mixture on unfinished table. Immediately wipe mixture off with clean, soft cloth. When dry, apply two coats of polyurethane. Let dry.

2 Measure table sides and draw design layout on paper. Starting ½ inch from table edge, plan two rows of 2-inch squares with nine tacks each. Use chalk line to mark placement lines on table.

3 Start setting tacks at any one corner. Hammer first three tacks along outside edge of first square. Next, hammer remaining corner tacks. This makes it easier to place center tacks. It is not necessary to measure center locations. Once corner tacks are set, hammer remaining tacks between them.

4 Each square requires nine upholstery tacks. Hammer center tack last. Work around table, filling each alternate square, one at a time, with tacks. Don't space them too far apart because design loses clarity. Once all tacks are in place, remove all chalk line marks with damp cloth.

BLOCKS OF FURNITURE COLOR

Energize furniture with these eclectic and bright color blocks that create a happy focal point.

BEFORE YOU BEGIN

To customize unfinished wooden furniture, create color blocks with motifs to match the color and design schemes in your home.

Planning the Design

For the most striking results, choose furniture with various elements—drawers, doors, panels and moldings—that lend themselves to color blocking. Keep in mind that painted knobs and pulls also add to the design.

Draw an outline of the furniture (below left) on scrap paper to plan the blocks. Using colored pencils, experiment with different color or pattern ideas for each drawer or door. Create more blocks by using two or more colors in one area.

Add patterns such as graphic stripes, crosses or flowers over the color blocks to create extra interest.

Use a photocopier to enlarge the flower (below) to the desired size. Then, transfer the template to cardboard and cut out.

Furniture Preparation

Use unfinished wood pieces or make over painted furniture by stripping and sanding the item. Before painting either, lightly sand wood, then wipe away sawdust with a damp cloth.

For best results, remove drawers and doors and place on a clean, flat surface to paint. Unscrew all hardware and set aside until furniture is painted.

Paint bright, primary colors directly onto an unfinished wood surface. For lighter shades, apply a coat of primer first.

COLOR-BLOCKING A CUPBOARD

1 Following your finished outline (Before You Begin), measure and mark color squares on door and drawer faces with a T square and pencil.

2 Align edges of painter's masking tape with pencil lines, marking off areas to paint first two colors. Press tape firmly to wood and cut tape.

3 With round paintbrush, apply an even coat of paint inside taped areas and let dry. Continue until all areas of same color are painted. Add extra coat if needed.

HANDY HINTS

Shop craft stores for stamps and stencils or copy a motif from fabric or wallpaper to coordinate the design with your decor.

QUICK FIX

To touch up uneven edges, place a ruler against the uneven line, then use a fine paintbrush to fill in paint. Carefully lift the ruler and let dry.

4 Once paint is dry, carefully lift tape. Cut new pieces of tape and mark off blocks for second paint color. With round paintbrush, apply paint inside taped areas.

5 Continue taping and painting for each paint color. Before painting blocks with patterns, lightly transfer templates to wood with pencil.

6 Using small paintbrush, paint flower center one color and flower petals a second. When dry, use round paintbrush to carefully paint wood square around flower.

7 Continue until all color blocks are painted. With sponge brush, paint around door panels, sides, top and trim on front. Paint knobs; let dry. Apply two coats of matte varnish to all areas. Reattach door and install drawers and hardware.

Stenciled Patterns that Coordinate Decor

Capitalize on the easy technique of stenciling to coordinate an entire room.

BEFORE YOU BEGIN

Connect furniture, fabrics and walls with the same design. Use spray paint to stencil walls and furniture; use a brush for stenciling on fabric.

Making the Templates

For each item to be decorated, you will need the templates below: two pears (one for doing the shading on the pears); a stem; and three leaves.

Enlarge the designs to desired size for copying onto acetate. Use large acetate sheets for stencils to protect the surface being painted from excess paint spray.

Determine and mark placement of designs, leaving about 3 inches between each pear set.

Tools for Stenciling

A stencil burner makes smooth lines and curves around a stencil easy to achieve by burning a fine line through the acetate. To use, place a piece of glass over the template and place a sheet of acetate over the glass.

Heat the burner to the temperature recommended by the manufacturer, then guide the tip of the burner around the stencil's outline.

A small spray gun is another tool that helps facilitate this project. The spray gun has better control than a spray can and is faster than stenciling with a brush.

Load the spray gun with acrylic paints to stencil designs on walls and wood furnishings. The paint may need to be diluted.

Keep the cord behind the spray gun during stenciling.

STENCILING FURNISHINGS WITH A SPRAY GUN

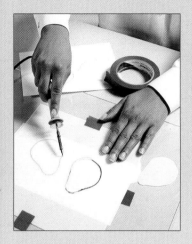

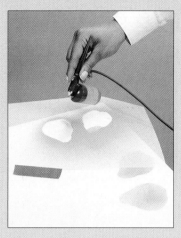

1 Cover template with a piece of glass. Place acetate over glass; tape in place. Using stencil burner, trace outlines of pears. Repeat on separate acetate sheets to make remaining three stencils (Before You Begin).

2 Working in a well-ventilated area, practice spray painting designs on paper before painting on furniture and walls. Experiment with shading pears and painting designs without saturating them with paint.

3 Tape pear stencil to mark on table (Before You Begin). Load spray gun with yellow paint, then spray even coat over pears; let dry. Continue around edge of table until all pears are painted. Allow to dry completely.

HANDY HINTS

Wash fabric and sheets before stenciling to remove the sizing.

Purchase a spray gun or stencil burner from a local craft store or hobby shop.

Clean the nozzle of the spray gun with mild detergent and warm water after each use to keep it from clogging with dried paint.

Expand your horizons with stencils other than the pears shown here.

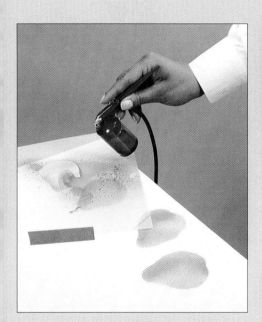

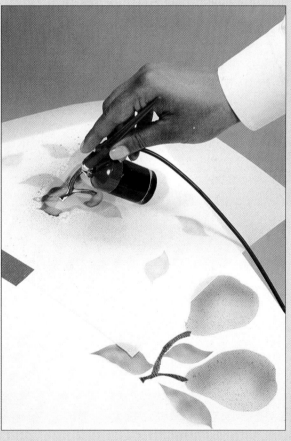

4 Tape stencil for shading over painted pears. Load spray gun with rust paint, then speckle pears with short, quick sprays to highlight; let dry. Reposition stencil and continue until all pears are shaded.

5 Tape stencil for leaves over pears. To create highlights in leaves, spray paint them with an uneven coat of green paint; let dry. Repeat around table. Create effect of falling leaves between each set of pears by turning leaf stencil in different directions and spraying one or two leaves; let dry. Then, tape stem stencil over pears. Spray paint stem with brown paint; repeat around table.

PERSONALIZED CABINETS AND DRAWERS

Hand-painted knobs and pulls add personality to a once-plain kitchen.

YOU WILL NEED

- ❏ WOODEN KNOBS OR PULLS
- ❏ ACRYLIC PAINTS
- ❏ PRIMER
- ❏ FINE-POINTED & SMALL, FLAT PAINTBRUSHES
- ❏ CLEAR VARNISH
- ❏ FINE-POINT, BLACK PERMANENT MARKER
- ❏ PENCIL

BEFORE YOU BEGIN

Decorating wooden knobs and pulls is not only simple and quick, but it is also an inexpensive way to dramatically change a cabinet's look.

Prep Work for Knobs

For best results, purchase knobs and pulls with flat fronts. Rounded, uneven surfaces can be tricky to paint or decorate.
• For new knobs, sand the wood before priming.
• For existing knobs, remove paint or varnish and sand smooth.

• Choose a simple design (below) to paint. You can transfer each one freehand or enlarge them on a photocopier and transfer the images using graphite paper.
• If you make an error, reapply the base coat.

Innovative Design Ideas

While almost any design is adaptable for decorating knobs or pulls, geometric shapes are the easiest designs to transfer and paint.

Let Mother Nature inspire your motifs. Leaves, flowers, fruits, celestial shapes (stars and moons) and vegetables are attractive themes for painting knobs.

Turn to your decor for ideas. Enlarge or reduce

patterns found in upholstery and decorator fabrics, china, rugs and wallpaper.

Faux finishes such as marbling, spatter painting and sponging are quick and easy to execute on the small surfaces of knobs and pulls.

Decoupage miniature cut-out paper designs or even family photographs in the center of painted knobs.

PAINTING DECORATIVE KNOBS

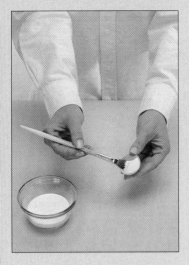

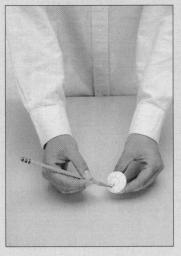

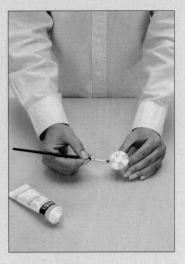

HANDY HINTS

For better control and sharper designs, use smaller brushes to paint the knobs and pulls.

For a quick base coat, eliminate priming and spray paint the knobs with several coats of the desired color of paint. Be sure to let the knobs dry between coats.

1 Prepare each knob (Before You Begin), then prime. To make the knobs easier to hold during the painting process, paint the tops first; let dry. Then hold each knob along the top and paint the sides and stem.

2 When dry, use a pencil to lightly draw the designs (Before You Begin) on the top of each knob. Select two or three bright paint colors that stand out next to each other and plan their placement within the designs.

3 Using the pencil lines as a guide, begin painting the lightest color first onto the knobs with a small, pointed paintbrush. Apply two coats of acrylic paint if necessary to produce clear, brilliant colors.

DOLLAR SENSE

To save money and shopping time, repaint the existing knobs and pulls on your cabinets. Simply remove the knobs, prep and then paint as desired. When dry, reattach knobs to the cabinets.

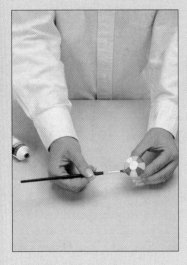

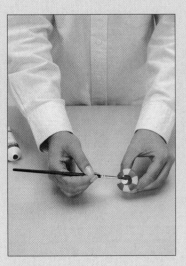

4 When the first paint color is dry, continue painting the designs with the second color. For support, hold the stem of the knob and steady your hands against a stable surface while painting to keep lines straight.

5 Finish painting all the colors of the design onto the knob. Allow the paint to dry, then touch up any crooked lines or uneven paint finishes. If each knob features a different design, complete each design; let dry.

6 With a fine-point, permanent black marker, outline the designs to create definition and to distinguish between the various colors. To finish, seal the tops and stems of all the knobs with a clear coat of varnish.

DECORATIVE WORDS ON FURNITURE

Simple phrases turn everyday furniture into endearing heirlooms.

YOU WILL NEED

- ❏ PAINTED WOODEN TABLE
- ❏ ACRYLIC PAINTS
- ❏ FINE PAINTBRUSH
- ❏ PENCIL
- ❏ PATTERN FOR LETTERS
- ❏ SPRAY ADHESIVE
- ❏ PAINTER'S MASKING TAPE
- ❏ PLAIN PAPER
- ❏ POLYURETHANE

BEFORE YOU BEGIN

When painting on furniture, choose words or phrases that reflect your personality or set a mood in a room.

Preparing the Surface

Working on a smoothly sanded and painted surface will help the letters adhere when transferring the markings to the table.

• Use a stripping compound to remove old coats of paint and varnish from the tabletop.

• Sand the surface smooth with a fine grade of sandpaper. Wipe away the dust with a soft, lint-free towel or cloth.

• Apply a coat of primer to the table. Once dry, apply two coats of paint.

• For a stained finish, sand the table as indicated, then apply stain with a soft-bristle paintbrush. Let the table dry completely before transferring the letters.

Enlarging Letters to Transfer

Choose a phrase or a saying. Then scout around for a style of lettering, or use a photocopier to enlarge the letters (right) until they are the desired size. If you select a different phrase or word(s), the alphabet below will help.

Cut out each letter using sharp scissors, then arrange them around the table to make sure they fit.

Use a spray mounting adhesive on the back of the letters for easy mounting and removing. This technique allows the letters to be arranged as desired. Using stencils can sometimes involve lengthy mathematical calculations.

LAUGHTER

IS THE

SHORTEST

DISTANCE

BETWEEN

TWO

PEOPLE

A B C D E F G H

I J K L M N O P

Q R S T U V W X

Y Z

PAINTING WORDS ON FURNITURE

OOPS

To touch up lettering mistakes, paint over the mistake with paint the color of the table. For stained surfaces, sand over the mistake and apply stain with a cotton swab.

1 To make the border, lightly draw four parallel lines around the edge of the table, 1½ inches, 1¾ inches, 4¼ inches and 4½ inches from the edge. Apply painter's tape to the outside and inside edges of the first two lines and press flat. Repeat for the remaining two lines.

2 Make sure the tape is pressed flat to the table without any air bubbles. Using a soft brush, paint over the surfaces exposed between the tapes. Let dry; then apply another coat. When paint has dried completely, remove tape.

3 Lay the letters around the table between the borders, spacing the letters equally in all words. When arranged as desired, lift each letter one at a time, coat the back with spray adhesive and press it flat onto the table's surface.

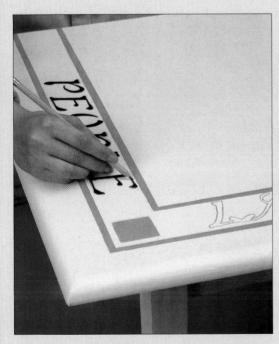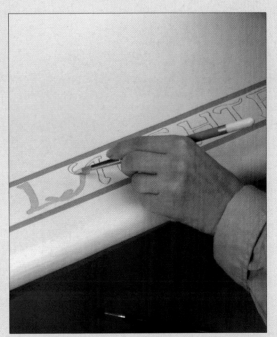

4 Using a pencil, lightly trace around each letter. When all of the letters have been transferred to the table, remove the letters by lifting one corner of a letter and carefully peeling it from the surface. Double check the spacing.

5 Using a fine paintbrush, fill in the lettering with paint. Work from left to right to prevent dragging your hand through painted letters. When dry, touch up each letter as needed. Seal the paint with two coats of polyurethane.

Innovative Papering on Furniture

Use decorative wallpaper accents to liven up faded furniture.

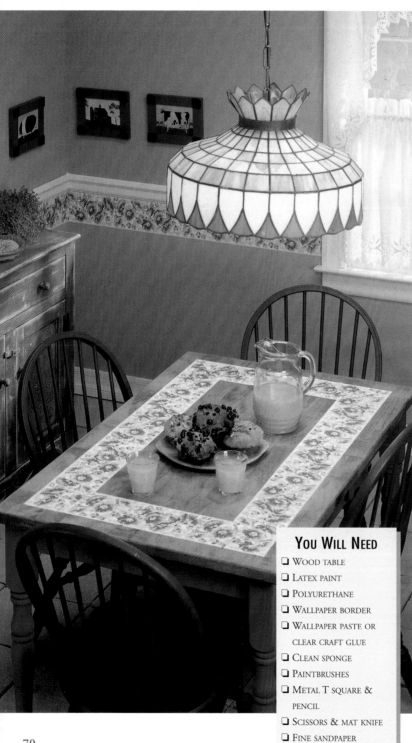

BEFORE YOU BEGIN

Whether you're applying paper to stained or painted wood, inspect the furniture carefully for blemishes and repair any imperfections before you apply decorative paper.

Preparing the Wood

For deep nicks or dents, fill in the space with wood putty, which is available in several shades to match the stained wood.

To remove old paint, use a chemical paint remover or a heat gun and scraper.

To maintain a smooth finish, sand the wood before and after applying the stain, to smooth the hair-like fibers. Always sand in the direction of the wood grain.

For a natural finish on new wood, apply equal parts alcohol and clear shellac to seal the wood without adding color.

To camouflage a deep scratch, color the area with matching wood stain applied with a toothpick. Alternatively, use a crayon or felt-tipped marker (below left).

To raise a shallow dent in stained wood, prick the deepest part of the dent in several areas. Cover with a damp towel. Press with a hot iron for a few seconds (below right).

Border Tips

• Wallpaper borders are available in a range of widths, from ¾ inch to 18 inches. Choose a width that suits the dimensions of your table.

• Use an architectural border to give the illusion of inlaid wood on a tabletop.
• Make your own borders from wallpaper remnants and use them to paper a tabletop to match a newly decorated room.

PAPERING THE FURNITURE

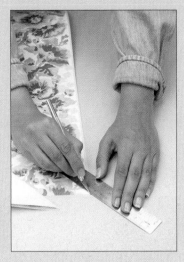

HANDY HINTS

Borders work best on tables with straight sides. If you want to decorate a round table, choose a narrow border and slash into its inner edge at ½-inch intervals. Then you can overlap the sections to turn the border around the curved edges.

1 Repair any dents and nicks in the wood surface, as described in Before You Begin. Apply primer to table legs; let dry. Paint the legs a color that complements the colors of the wallpaper border.

2 Measure the border width. Using a T square and pencil, mark the placement of the border on top of the table; set it about 4 inches from the edges of the table. Lightly sand the area of the table to be papered.

3 Measure and cut the border to fit each side of the table; allow extra for mitering. Position the dominant motif in the center of each side. Use a craft knife and straightedge to miter the ends of each strip at a 45° angle.

5 Using warm water and a sponge, wipe away all excess glue or paste from top of paper and table. Allow paper to dry thoroughly for at least 24 hours. Apply two or three coats of polyurethane finish to the tabletop. Sand and wipe clean between each layer with steel wool and a soft, lint-free cloth.

4 Using wallpaper paste or clear craft glue, apply the wallpaper border to the table along marked line. Follow the wallpaper manufacturer's instructions for pasting over painted or stained surfaces.

Easy Shutter Screens

Make easy-to-assemble room divider screens from shutters.

BEFORE YOU BEGIN

Painting the shutters before attaching the shelves makes this project much more straightforward. For a more interesting yet still subtle look, paint the shutters and shelves two different, but complementary, shades of the same color.

Painting the Shutters

Spray paint makes it easy to decorate shutters with louvers or intricate details. Compare the expense of spray paint to brush paint by calculating the coverage listed on the back of the can. Always use spray paint outside or in a well-ventilated room.

For an unusual look, consider using spray paints that imitate the appearance of granite or stone.

If using latex paint, apply several thin coats for better coverage and to avoid excessive buildup. Try to choose a paint with a gloss finish to eliminate fingerprints on shutters that may be moved or handled frequently.

Finish with a couple of coats of clear polyurethane if extra protection is needed.

Position shutters for painting and finishing on a vertical or horizontal work surface. The shutters should be easily accessible from all sides so that paint drips can be caught quickly; this is especially important for louvered shutters. Set up an old table or sawhorses for a work surface that's easy on the knees and back. Protect the floor from paint drips by covering it with newspaper or plastic (below).

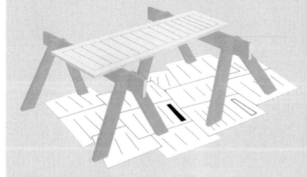

Using Hinges

- A hinge consists of a center pin and two jambs. Diameter of pin will determine space left between two shutters.
- To position hinges, jamb must be flat against sides of shutter and central pin must extend past back edge of shutter.
- For an accordion-fold screen, alternate pin position so that it faces front on first pair of shutters then back on second pair, etc.

ASSEMBLING THE SCREEN

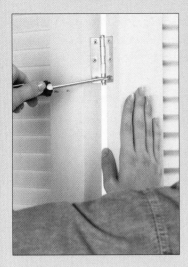

1 Mark hinge location on edges of shutters. Position top and bottom hinges 4 inches from short ends; position third hinge in middle. Mark location of screw holes. Screw hinge to shutter (see Before You Begin).

2 Cut shelf equal to shutter width; sand ends. Apply wood glue to top of one bracket. Position bracket on underside of shelf, ½ inch from one short end; hold in place for a few seconds. Repeat at other end of shelf.

3 When wood glue has dried completely, hammer finishing nails through top of shelf into bracket. Apply wood putty to camouflage nail hole; sand when dry. Repeat Steps 2 and 3 with remaining shelves.

4 When all brackets have been attached to shelves, prime, paint and seal shelf assemblies in a color that harmonizes with shutters. Remember that undersides of shelves must be painted too.

5 Mark bracket position on borders of shutters. Attach two mounting hooks to back of each shelf and two nails to marks on each shutter; nails must be slightly shorter than shutter depth. Slot hooks over nails to mount shelves.

SPONGE-PAINTED FURNITURE

Create unique pieces by sponge painting over flea market finds.

YOU WILL NEED

- ❏ LATEX PAINT
- ❏ MEDIUM-SIZE SEA SPONGES
- ❏ SANDPAPER & STEEL WOOL
- ❏ WOOD PUTTY OR SPACKLING COMPOUND
- ❏ LATEX GLOVES
- ❏ NEWSPAPER
- ❏ MIXING BUCKETS
- ❏ POLYURETHANE
- ❏ PAINTBRUSH

BEFORE YOU BEGIN

Check flea markets, attics and garages for old pieces of furniture that you can transform into contemporary treasures.

Transforming Furniture

First check the condition of old furniture when eyeing its potential. If repairs will be easy, look beyond the surface flaws and imagine how the item will look sponge painted.

• Loose joints and small cracks and scratches are very easy to repair.

• Don't take on a project if the furniture is unsound and terribly worn.

Rediscover the value of old chairs that have been abandoned in the garage or the attic for years (below). The styles and finishes of the chairs don't even have to match because the sponging treatment will work to tie them all together.

Sponge Painting Tricks

Sponging with latex paint creates this look (below left). Each layer of paint completely covers the layer underneath it. Latex is the easiest type of paint to use on furniture, but you should apply a protective coating over it to prevent smudges and scratches.

Sponging with paint glaze creates a translucent, shiny finish. With glaze sponging, you can see through the glaze colors to the colors underneath (below right). Latex paint is used for the base color and two glaze colors are applied on top.

 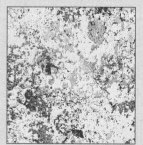

74

SPONGE PAINTING A CHAIR

HANDY HINTS

Make sure one paint color dries thoroughly before applying another one. Sponging while the first color is still wet will make the colors merge and smear.

QUICK FIX

If there is too much of a sponged color for your liking, sponge over it with a bit of the base coat to lighten the look.

1 To begin, sand the chair with a medium- or fine-grade sandpaper. Use steel wool on irregular surfaces like carvings and chair legs. Brush off remaining grit and putty from any areas that need it.

2 Paint one coat of the base color. Although sponging will cover a lot, two coats of paint may be needed if the surface is dark or badly mottled. Allow each coat of paint to dry before proceeding.

3 Dilute paint to consistency of heavy cream. Put on latex gloves and sponge on first color. Soak entire sponge in paint, squeeze out excess and blot on paper. Use a pouncing motion and rotate the sponge.

4 Once paint is completely dry, sponge on the second color. Use a different sponge to introduce a new color and pattern. Hold sponge lightly and work from wrist. Randomly sponge to cover entire surface.

5 Step back often to check the effect; the final color is always the strongest. Then decide whether the base color or the sponging color(s) should dominate and sponge on more paint as necessary.

6 Once all the paint layers are dry, brush on a protective finish coat of polyurethane. Check hardware stores for a non-yellowing formula. Then clean sponges in warm, soapy water and let them dry.

A Slipcover for Straight-Back Chairs

A slipcover in country checks makes a formal chair more casual.

YOU WILL NEED

- ❏ FABRIC
- ❏ CORDING OR PIPING
- ❏ ½-INCH-WIDE TWILL TAPE
- ❏ SEWING MACHINE
- ❏ THREAD
- ❏ MEASURING TAPE
- ❏ SCISSORS

BEFORE YOU BEGIN

Record the measurements below to determine the amount of fabric to purchase and to ensure a good fit.

Measuring

Required measurements:
- A: length of chair back
- B: width of chair back, width of chair front
- C: length of chair front and seat
- D: width and depth of chair seat
- E: height of chair seat

For cording length, add B + 2A + 2D + 12 inches

Pleat Allowance

Before purchasing fabric, determine desired number and placement of pleats around chair seat. A good rule of thumb is to have an equal number of pleats on each chair side and an equal number of pleats on chair front and back. For each pleat, add at least 8 inches of fabric to the width of the skirt. Use the diagram below as a guide for folding the pleats into place.

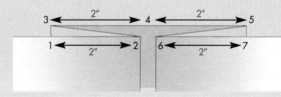

Cutting Fabric

The necessary fabric yardage depends on the dimensions of your chair and the size of fabric repeat using the diagram and measurements above:
- 1 chair back (AxB)
- 1 chair front/seat (CxB)
- 1 skirt ([2D + total pleat allowance] x [E + 1-inch hem])

Before cutting, add ½-inch seam allowances to all edges except hem edge of skirt. Fabric pieces must be seamed to achieve necessary skirt width. Stitch skirt pieces together to form a continuous circle. Do not press seams open.

SEWING THE SLIPCOVER

1 Mark pleats along skirt upper and lower edges (Before You Begin), on right side of fabric. Pin all marks 2 inches apart. Mark 7 for pleat one will also be mark 1 for pleat two. Continue around the skirt.

2 Right side up, bring marks 2 and 6 to meet at mark 4; marks 3 and 1 and marks 5 and 7 should align with each other. Press in place from top to bottom; baste ³⁄₈ inch from upper edge. Continue pleating skirt.

3 Right side up, pin cording to sides and top of seat back aligning raw edges. Pin the back and front right sides together at top and side edges. Stitch ½ inch from edge, leaving ½ inch open at base of side seams.

HANDY HINTS

When stitching seams with cording trim, using a zipper foot on the sewing machine will make the job quicker and easier.

TAKE NOTE

Don't forget necessary seam allowances and the length of pattern repeats when planning fabric yardage.

4 Right side up, pin the cording to outer edge of seat front, sides and back. Start at center back, overlapping raw edges and tapering them into seam allowance. Stitch cording just inside the seam line.

5 Pin upper edge of chair skirt to the chair seat, front and back, with right sides facing. Center one skirt seam at center back. Stitch through all layers, ½ inch from edge, so cording stitching is in seam allowance.

6 For hem, turn in ½ inch at lower edge of skirt; press. Turn another ½ inch; press. Stitch hem in place; press pleats. For seat ties, cut two 20-inch pieces of twill tape. Fold each piece in half. On inside of chair cover, tack folded end to each side seam of seat back. Place cover over chair, and tie tapes to each side of chair back.

ANTIQUED WOODEN FURNITURE

Replicate the look of an antique with this simple paint technique.

BEFORE YOU BEGIN

Turn an ordinary piece of furniture into a collector's item with this simple painting and sanding technique.

Preparing the Furniture

Prepare the cupboard carefully before applying the colored paint.
- Remove all door hinges and handles.
- For previously treated wood, clean with warm, soapy water to remove dirt and dust. Then sand lightly to remove peeling paint and varnish and to create a smooth surface. Wipe down again with a damp cloth; let dry. Apply a coat of primer.
- For unfinished wood, sand lightly and apply a coat of acrylic primer.

Where to Sand

When sanding off the topcoat of paint, pay particular attention to areas that would normally receive the most wear. For cupboards, this is generally on handles and around the edges of doors and panels.

When sanding wooden chairs to give them an antique look, emphasize the top back rail to give the appearance of years of handling. Also concentrate on the seat area and the bottom of the legs to imitate the knocks and scrapes that may have built up from shoes over the years.

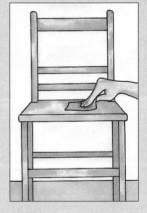

A Glazed Look

Antiquing glaze contains raw umber acrylic paint which tones down modern colors to give them an aged look. The basic formula for antiquing glaze is 2 tablespoons raw umber acrylic paint to 1 cup latex glaze. However, the glaze color depends on the color of the topcoat: the darker the paint, the darker the glaze needs to be.

ANTIQUING THE CUPBOARD

1 Work on cupboard door first. Apply one coat of green paint over white primer. Allow to dry completely. Always choose a base color that contrasts with the primer for a more obvious look of layers of paint.

2 Sand off paint randomly, concentrating mainly on areas of normal wear so primer coat and bare wood show through. For large jobs, use an electric sander instead of a sandpaper block.

3 Test glaze on inside of furniture to be sure color is satisfactory. Then apply glaze with foam brush, working on one small area at a time. Glaze will be cloudy at first, but will become clear as it dries.

HANDY HINTS

To make antiqued furniture look even more authentic, add fake woodworm holes using a drill with an extra-fine bit after the final coat of paint has been applied

QUICK FIX

If you are not satisfied with the piece, simply sand more, then apply more paint to fix oversanding or reapply a different shade of glaze.

4 Wipe off glaze with a clean, damp cloth. Keep in mind areas of normal wear and tear; leave more glaze in grooves to give wood an aged effect. Once desired effect is achieved, seal with a coat of polyurethane.

5 Repeat painting, sanding and glazing process on rest of cupboard. Pay special attention to legs and corners. Make sure color of doors matches rest of piece. When desired effect is achieved and all wood is dry, replace hinges and doors.

Easy Marbling Effects on Wood

Transform old furniture with easy and elegant marbling effects.

You Will Need

- ❏ White eggshell paint
- ❏ Oil-based glaze
- ❏ Artist's oil paints
- ❏ Soft-bristled brush, fine artist's brush, stippling brush & paintbrush
- ❏ Mineral spirits
- ❏ Polyurethane varnish
- ❏ Wood putty
- ❏ Sandpaper (rough & fine)
- ❏ Empty jelly jars

BEFORE YOU BEGIN

Plan before painting. Pencil in the veining pattern on a large piece of paper and practice painting lines to see what the effect will look like.

Preparing the Surface

Rub down varnished or painted surfaces with rough quality sandpaper. Fill any cracks or dents with wood putty—a flat surface is essential as glaze will pool in any hollows. Allow filler to harden, then sand surface again with fine quality paper for a smooth finish.

Wipe the surface with a damp cloth to ensure that it is completely dust free. Apply two coats of white eggshell paint. This not only acts as a primer but also creates an evenly colored surface that will show off the marbling colors and patterns to best advantage.

Preparing the Glaze

Prepare one cup of diluted glaze—two parts glaze to one part mineral spirits—and mix well. Pour into two jars (one for pink, one for black). Dilute pink artist's oil paint with a little mineral spirits and mix into one of the jars of prepared glaze. Repeat with the black paint.

MARBLING ON WOOD

1 Apply pink glaze with a paintbrush using rough strokes in a variety of directions. Make definite strokes, but be careful not to make splashes by overloading the brush with paint.

2 Soften the pink strokes by dabbing them with a clean cloth. Then use a fairly wide, soft brush to create new strokes with less distinct but still visible directional lines.

3 Using the already mixed, medium-strength black glaze, paint a series of shaky diagonal lines, varying the thickness while painting to give the veins a rough, uneven look.

HANDY HINTS

Varied width of strokes and a slightly shaky hand are the keys to creating realistic marbled lines. Coloring the basic black glaze with deep green, blue or red helps to give the overall effect a greater depth of tone and realism.

4 Dab a stippling brush or other wide, blunt brush over the wet paint to blur the veins and make them softer looking. Use varying pressure to give the lines extra interest.

5 Add more black paint to the glaze to make it a stronger color. Apply new veins roughly along the middle of the first ones. Soften with a stippling brush after five minutes.

OOPS

Any mistakes can easily be corrected by cleaning off the area with a dab of mineral spirits on a clean dish towel and then repainting.

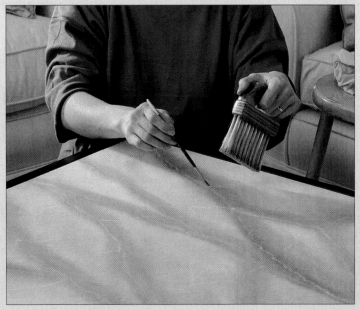

6 Use an artist's brush dipped in mineral spirits to draw small veins in the opposite direction of black veins, removing some glaze in the process.

7 Create a rough overall effect of elongated diamonds with the artist's brush. As a finishing touch, soften the mineral spirits lines with a clean stippling brush, being careful not to remove the paint.

FABRIC-COVERED SCREENS

Attractively divide a room with a screen covered to fit the setting.

YOU WILL NEED
- ❏ SCREEN
- ❏ FABRIC & WOVEN BRAID
- ❏ COTTON BATTING
- ❏ STAPLE GUN & STAPLES
- ❏ UPHOLSTERY TACKS
- ❏ HAMMER OR RUBBER MALLET
- ❏ GLUE GUN & GLUE STICKS
- ❏ MEASURING TAPE
- ❏ CHALK

BEFORE YOU BEGIN

Staple batting and fabric to a wood screen to create a functional furnishing that looks like it was customed designed and created.

Determining Amounts

Mark the screen area to be covered with fabric. Leave at least 2 inches of wood trim showing at each edge.

Measure finished area for fabric cover, adding 4 inches to both height and width. Multiply this amount by the number of screen panels. Double if covering back. If using a print fabric, buy extra so repeat starts in same place on each screen panel.

Cut fabric to size. Then fold under to create a 2-inch hem along each edge and press.

With chalk, mark the center of the top, bottom and sides of the screen and of the fabric. Then match the chalk

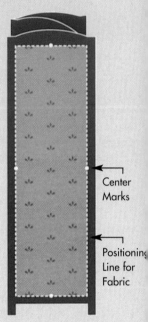

Center Marks

Positioning Line for Fabric

points to position the fabric on the screen (above).

Finding the Right Trim

Place trim around the edge to cover staples. Trim can be found at sewing and home decorating stores in a variety of widths, textures and colors. See some examples below.

When buying trim, measure the circumference of the fabric area and add 4 inches for turning corners.

STAPLING FABRIC TO A SCREEN

HANDY HINTS

If the screen has a hollow center, apply fabric to back of screen before stapling two or three layers of batting to front of screen. This will protect batting, hold it in place, and conceal it from the rear.

DOLLAR SENSE

Cut an old flat sheet to cover a screen at almost no expense. Or get an extra flat sheet when buying bed linen for a coordinated look in a bedroom.

1 Cut batting to size of finished area and staple batting to screen at exact location for fabric cover. Use only a few staples to hold batting in place. If using several layers, staple each separately.

2 Staple top center of fabric to top center marking on frame. Stretch fabric so it covers batting snugly and staple bottom center to frame. Be sure pattern is accurately positioned if there are repeats.

3 Working toward the corners, one side at a time, staple the upper edge of the fabric to frame. Be sure to keep any pattern even at the top. Repeat along the lower edge, keeping fabric stretched.

4 Again working toward the corners, one side at a time, staple sides of the fabric panel to sides of the frame. Make sure the fabric is snugly stretched and keep any pattern repeats evenly positioned.

5 Cut braid to cover an entire panel. Starting at a lower corner, center braid over staples. Use hot glue to hold braid in place. Work in small amounts so glue does not dry before braid is affixed.

6 Add upholstery tacks for a formal decorative effect. Use a rubber mallet—or a hammer covered with several layers of cloth—to hammer upholstery tacks into the screen through the braid and the fabric.

DON'T FORGET
WALLS, DOORS & FLOORS

If there are forgotten cousins in any decorating scheme, it's usually the walls, doors and floors … and often all three. A coat of paint takes care of a wall or door, a nice rug hides the floor, then you're free to pursue more "exciting" decorating plans. But walls, doors and floors present almost endless opportunities to decorate with grace, style, taste and excitement. Special painting techniques and effects are the norm here, but you'll find plenty of other great and easy-to-implement ideas as well. Time to give those walls, doors and floors some much-deserved attention. Don't forget them!

DECORATIVE RELIEF WALLCOVERINGS

Panels of sculpted wallpaper lend classic elegance to a formal decor.

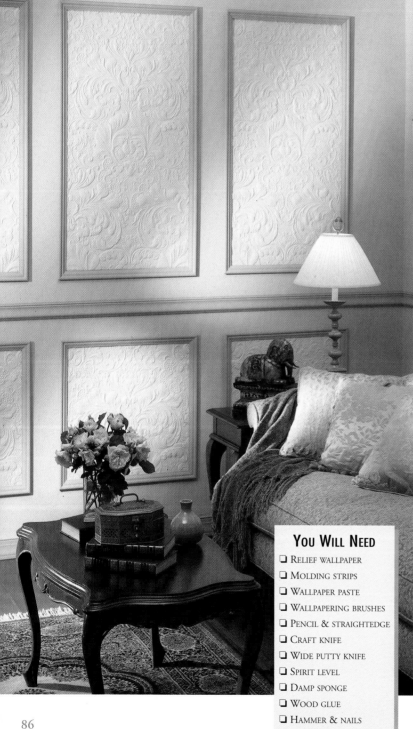

YOU WILL NEED

- ❏ RELIEF WALLPAPER
- ❏ MOLDING STRIPS
- ❏ WALLPAPER PASTE
- ❏ WALLPAPERING BRUSHES
- ❏ PENCIL & STRAIGHTEDGE
- ❏ CRAFT KNIFE
- ❏ WIDE PUTTY KNIFE
- ❏ SPIRIT LEVEL
- ❏ DAMP SPONGE
- ❏ WOOD GLUE
- ❏ HAMMER & NAILS

BEFORE YOU BEGIN

Look for textured wallpaper designs that suit the style of the room.

Papering Tips

• Decorative relief wallpaper comes in many designs. Some patterns are very ornate and sophisticated (1), making them perfect for formal rooms; others feature simpler, often geometric, designs which are great for casual decor (2 and 3).

• Instead of using a roller to press the seams to the wall, tap them with a spreading brush instead. A roller will just crush the relief design.

1
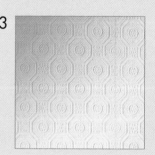

2
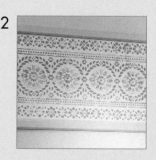

3

HANGING DECORATIVE RELIEF WALLPAPER

1 Plan how many wallpaper panels will fit on wall with equal spaces between them. Draw pencil lines to show positioning of top, bottom and side edges of panels. Use a spirit level to ensure straight lines.

2 Mark cutting line lightly in pencil on back of paper, so that line lies at right angle with edges. Use craft knife to cut strips to desired length.

3 Paste first strip; fold both ends into middle. Roll loosely; let sit for 10 minutes. Unfold top section and position so edge is parallel to vertical line.

HANDY HINTS

Textured wallpaper can be used to camouflage any flaws and imperfections in the surface of a wall.

DOLLAR SENSE

Panels of textured wallpaper produce the same classic look as a completely papered wall, but at less than half the cost.

4 Unfold remaining section of wallpaper strip and press into place on wall, taking care not to stretch or crush paper. Adjust placement of strip if necessary, using vertical and horizontal pencil lines as a guide.

5 Smooth paper flat with a spreading brush, fanning out from center to edges. Carefully remove all air bubbles. Tap edges gently with spreading brush to ensure they lie perfectly flat against wall.

6 Make sure wallpaper is securely pasted to wall, especially around edges. Wipe off wallpaper strip and surrounding wall with a damp sponge to remove excess adhesive. Rinse sponge and squeeze out as needed. Repeat Steps 3-6 to apply remaining wallpaper strips.

7 Cut molding strips to desired length, mitering ends at a 45° angle. Use wood glue and nails to fix molding in place around edges of each wallpaper panel, making sure corners fit together neatly.

DECOUPAGE WALLS

For a contemporary look, accent windows with floral paper strips.

BEFORE YOU BEGIN

Decoupage, from the French word meaning "to cut," requires a pair of small, sharp scissors and a collection of charming designs on paper.

Thematic Pictures

Decoupage material is best selected on the basis of the room's overall theme.
• For a child's room, look in books of nursery rhymes and animal stories, or use whimsical wrapping paper or greeting cards.

• Music lovers can use a favorite sheet of music for the master image.
• For a kitchen or breakfast room, try colorful pictures of fruits and vegetables.
• For traditional rooms, images from books and journals are good sources.

Planning the Layout

Proper spacing of any decoupage design is dependent upon the size of the pattern, pattern repeat and the space to be filled. A solid border is relatively easy to position. Simply cut all sections to the same measure and align them precisely. However, motifs that "float freely" require additional planning (below):
• Find the horizontal by measuring up or down from an existing straight edge such as a windowsill or baseboard. Pencil in a faint line to indicate placement

of the top or bottom of the cutouts.
• Find the center of the horizontal line and tack up the first cutout with drafting tape.
• Calculate the number of pattern repeats needed to fill the remaining spaces.
• Tape the repeat cutouts at regular intervals, adjusting them ever so slightly until a satisfying balance both horizontally and vertically is achieved.
• Faintly mark the wall and cutouts so they match up when pasted.

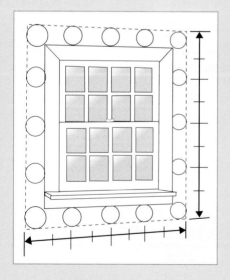

CUTTING AND APPLYING DECOUPAGE

1 Choose a paper, such as a printed napkin, with colors and design features that coordinate with the room. Trim away excess paper. Hold the scissors in a relaxed manner and carefully cut around the design.

2 Tack the cut pieces in place with drafting tape according to the desired layout. Mark the wall and the cutouts with positioning guides to ensure a proper alignment. Carefully remove the drafting tape.

3 Prepare the adhesive for the paper cutouts, using three parts white glue and one part water. Mix in a small bowl or a disposable plastic saucer. Make sure the glue and water mixture is consistently smooth.

TAKE NOTE

Select designs with bold edges that lend themselves to being cut out neatly. Avoid lacy images unless they come precut, as in the case of paper doilies.

OOPS

If you cut into the paper design by mistake, not to worry. Just be extra careful when pasting the cutout to realign the edges of the design as they were originally.

4 Working in small sections, dip a sponge brush in the glue and spread it thinly on the designated wall surface. Position the cutout on the wall according to positioning guides.

5 Working from the center outward, press it in place with a dry sponge and your fingers. Work quickly, as there is about a minute before the glue sets. Take special care to squeeze out air bubbles and excess glue for a smooth finish. Allow the paper to dry for a few minutes while continuing on to the next section of the design. Clean up any remaining residue with a slightly damp sponge.

NEW LOOKS FOR LATTICE

Bring lattice inside and dress it up to make a creative backdrop.

BEFORE YOU BEGIN

Hanging lattice over ordinary spaces creates architectural interest in places that have none. Experiment by cutting the lattice into various sizes and then propping or hanging it against the wall.

Creative Uses for Lattice

Originally designed for outdoor use, lattice is becoming a popular material to use inside. Consider lattice when challenged with decorating dilemmas.

The low cost and relative ease in working with lattice makes it ideal for quick home improvement projects. Most lattice projects take no longer than a day to complete. Generally, the most complex projects require only a weekend.

Lattice is available in various styles. The slats can be shaped into interesting images, the wood itself can be filigreed, or the slats can run perpendicular to each other.

When a room is lacking architectural interest, lattice can make an impact. Position it against walls, on the ceiling or around windows.

Adding a lattice window (below left) to hide an unsightly view is simple. Frame lattice with 1 by 4s on the top and sides; add a simple windowsill at the bottom.

Instead of wallpapering, cover the wall with lattice, and add molding to form a chair rail (below right).

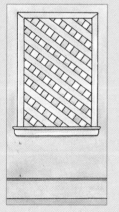

Buying Lattice

Lattice is available by the sheet at most hardware stores. It is usually made of a rough grade of 1-inch-wide wood.
• Transport lattice flat. The slats can break if the sheet is bent.

• Check lattice to make sure the nails or staples are flush with the wood, and that the ends are cut off evenly.
• For quick jobs, use prepainted lattice or molded acrylic lattice.

MAKING A LATTICE WALL

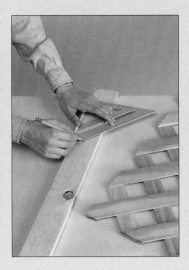

HANDY HINTS

Before working with lattice, lightly sand the slats for a better finish and a professional look.

1 Measure and cut the 1 by 4 into the four frame sides that will cover the lattice edges. Using a ruler and pencil, miter the corners by drawing a 45° angle at the ends of each piece. Cut the angle with a handsaw.

2 Nail the bottom piece of the frame to the lattice. Fit a frame side piece to the bottom piece at the joint. Nail together using brads. Continue around the lattice, securing joints and nailing the frame to the lattice.

3 Cover a flat surface with newspaper or a dropcloth. Place the lattice on top, with right side facing up. Paint the front and sides of the lattice. Let dry; then add a second coat of paint, if desired.

TAKE NOTE

To give hanging lattice more support, add a 1- by 4-inch piece of wood across the center. Paint it the same color as the rest of the lattice.

Spray painting is a quick alternative to painting with a brush. Prop the lattice against a support and coat with spray paint.

4 Lean the framed lattice piece against the wall to determine best placement. When the appropriate level and space is chosen, nail the lattice to the wall with finishing nails. Cover the nail holes with wood putty and paint, if desired.

Whimsical Touches for Doors and Trim

When you add a lighthearted touch, doors and trim become colorful canvases.

You Will Need

- ❏ Latex paints & primer
- ❏ Polyurethane
- ❏ Artist's paintbrush
- ❏ Foam brush
- ❏ Sandpaper
- ❏ Pencil & marker
- ❏ Craft scissors
- ❏ Acetate paper
- ❏ Screwdriver

BEFORE YOU BEGIN

Before starting the painting process, allow some time for careful preparation and planning. Taking time at the beginning makes the work go more smoothly.

Preparing the Surface

It is important to prepare the cabinet surface before beginning the project to ensure a quality job.
- Remove the hinges and doors with a screwdriver.
- Sand the entire cabinet with medium sandpaper, then follow up with fine sandpaper. If there are several layers of old paint on the piece and you see evidence of chipping or flaking, strip the cabinet down to the bare wood.
- Fill any cracks or nail holes with wood filler.
- Wipe the surface clean with a soft cloth.
- Apply a coat of white primer to all surfaces and allow to dry.

Drawing a Template

Using a photocopier, enlarge the large vine template (a) several times until it is of a scale that fits the dimensions of the cabinet doors. One vine should be centered on each cabinet door.

Follow the above copying directions for the smaller vine template (b). This template needs to be enlarged until it fits the vertical dimensions of the cabinet frame.

To extend a design, make multiple copies of the template. Lay the copies in sequence until there are enough repeats of the design to fill the available space from the top to the bottom of the cabinet area.

For the horizontal design lines on the cabinet frame, copy the vine template without the leaves (c) on a copy machine until it is enlarged to the desired size.

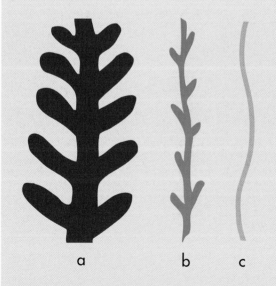

a   b   c

APPLYING THE MOTIFS

1 Transfer the vine template (Before You Begin) to a sheet of acetate with a marker. Using craft scissors, cut out the design by turning the acetate with a free hand and cutting continuously in one direction.

2 Position the cabinet door on a flat surface and place the acetate on top of it. Align properly and secure it with tape. With a pencil, trace the design to transfer it to the cabinet door. Remove the template.

3 Holding the artist's brush like a pencil, fill in the outlined vine shape. Be sure to curve the strokes, particularly along the edges of the design. Allow the paint to dry.

HANDY HINTS

Use a superior brush to achieve a strong, firm line when painting. The best choice is a brush of synthetic bristles specifically recommended for use with latex paints.

Remember, the goal is to keep a lighthearted look of whimsy. Don't belabor brush strokes; let creative expression flow in your strokes.

4 With a clean brush, paint the background around the vine red. Paint up to the edges of the vine to completely cover the primer. Reversing the vine and background colors, paint the other cabinet door.

5 Paint the cabinet frame in a compatible yellow; let dry. Using a pencil, transfer the templates of the smaller-scaled vine stems (Before You Begin) along the outside frame. Fill in the designs with green and red paints; let dry. Apply two coats of clear polyurethane with a small foam brush.

DESIGNS WITH CARPET TILES

Create a unique floor design when covering a floor with carpet tiles.

BEFORE YOU BEGIN

Finding a rug in the colors, design and price range you want can be difficult. Covering a floor with carpet tiles is the ideal solution to achieve the desired effect.

Choosing Carpet

Rubber backing on tiles holds the carpet's pile together during cutting. Look for tiles that have the same type of pile to produce a seamless effect when pieces are joined together.

Use a new, sharp blade to cut the carpet tiles. Always work with a metal straight-edge to avoid cutting mistakes. Cut from the back of the tile, always cutting away from yourself.

Pattern Play

Geometric designs are the easiest patterns to create with square carpet tiles.
• Plan your pattern on graph paper to determine the number of tiles needed for each color. Once a design has been established, mark the design cutting lines on the back of the tiles. Remember when marking on the back that you should mark the pattern in a mirror image because you are working on the reverse side of the tile.

• For round or curved designs, cut a template from a piece of plywood or cardboard. Lay the template on the back of the carpet tile and cut out with a utility knife. Always cut from the back of the tile to avoid ruining the pile.
• When choosing colors, keep in mind that dark colors are the easiest to keep clean. Complementary colors create high contrast, while shades in the same color family are subtle.

CUTTING THE CARPET TILES

1 Using a long metal ruler and a sharp utility knife, score lightly along the pattern drawn on the back of the carpet tile. Continue scoring along the line until the cut is all the way through the carpet.

2 Begin in one corner of the room and apply vinyl tile adhesive with a trowel; follow the manufacturer's instructions. Work in small sections, pulling the trowel in one direction for an even coat of adhesive.

3 Referring to the pattern (Before You Begin), begin laying carpet tiles on the floor, flush with the walls. Fit the next tile tightly against the first. Continue adding tiles until the section is covered.

4 Using a wallpaper roller, roll over edges of each carpet tile to ensure good adhesion. Pay particular attention to areas where several tiles meet. Allow at least 24 hours of drying time before moving furniture onto the floor.

DECORATIVE FLOOR BORDERS

Heighten visual interest underfoot with an easy-to-create border.

BEFORE YOU BEGIN

Brighten a sunroom with a cheerful floor border that resembles a length of colorful, stylized ribbon looping along and parallel to the baseboard.

Make a Stencil

Enlarge the stencil (left) to 7 inches wide, or to the desired size, with a photocopier. Print several copies.

Or, create your own stencil. Wallpaper, fabric or a pattern copied from a room accessory can become the takeoff point for stencil designs. Look for simple motifs that make impact through repetition, or modify the design for a stencil.

To check alignment, bend the photocopied design into a continuous loop and make sure that the ends match up nicely. Or, butt several copies end to end to see how they look.

Cover the photocopied design with stencil paper.

With a medium-tip felt-tipped marker, trace the design onto stencil paper. Use a straightedge or ruler to keep the long areas of the borders smooth and even.

Coordinating Colors

Before actually painting the stencil onto the floor, experiment with different combinations of coordinating or contrasting stencil colors.

Make several photocopies of the proposed design. Then color in the design with various pairings of markers or crayons to gauge the effect.

STENCILING A FLOOR BORDER

HANDY HINTS

Spray-mount adhesive comes in an aerosol can and provides a light, tacky backing suitable for many paper-based art projects. It's available at craft and art supply stores. Read the label to make sure the type you purchase allows items to be repositioned and does not immediately bond materials permanently to the surface.

1 Put the stencil paper (Before You Begin) on top of a mat or cutting board to protect the table. Using a sharp craft knife, cut out the design. Press firmly, making the strokes as long as possible to keep the borders smooth.

2 To plan the pattern repeat in the corner of the floor, lay two photocopies of the design perpendicular to one another on the floor and adjust placement as necessary. Mark placement around the room.

3 With a pencil, mark guide-lines on the floor to indicate placement for the edge of the stencil. Follow the marks around the perimeter of the floor with painter's masking tape, keeping the border straight.

4 Lightly coat the back of the stencil corners, or the corre-sponding spot on the floor, with repositionable spray-mount adhesive so the stencil will not slip during painting. Or, affix the stencil with masking tape.

5 For the ribbons, dip a stencil brush into blue paint, dab-bing off excess paint on a piece of scrap paper. Gently dab the blue ribbon areas, using a soft pouncing motion. Repeat with the remaining colors.

6 Lift the stencil from the completed area, being sure not to smudge the paint. If necessary, wipe off the back of the stencil to remove paint drips. Carefully reposition the stencil to the next spot on the floor. Protect the completed, dry floor with at least two coats of polyurethane.

ARTFUL WALLS

Create your own art exhibit with decorative wallpaper frames.

BEFORE YOU BEGIN

To form vignettes for your wall, group separate pieces of art together within a specific shape to make a unified composition.

Grouping Items for Display

Before applying wallpaper frames to the wall, lay all plates and/or pictures you wish to use in the composition on a flat surface. Be sure to include the width of the wallpaper, plus 3 inches for spacing, in the arrangement.

Enhance the grouping with an arrangement that contrasts the individual shapes of the frames—for example, a geometric cross-shaped grouping for oval plates (1).

For a more symmetrical grouping, use only frames or plates of the same size and shape to form a triangle (2). Vary the height of each piece for interest.

To mix various sizes and shapes, place items in an L-shaped arrangement (3). Position larger pieces first, then balance gaps with the smaller pieces.

Once you decide on an arrangement, use a soft pencil to lightly trace around the perimeter of each plate or picture frame to finalize its placement on the wall.

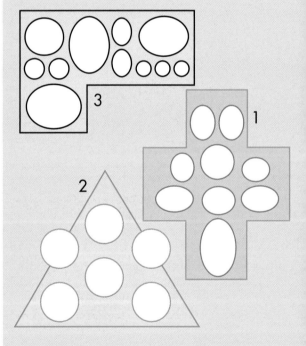

Frame Ideas

Consider these options for wallpaper borders:
- Hang a decorative strip of wallpaper in the center of a wall, then position framed pieces above and below.
- Apply a fancy border of wallpaper around an entire grouping of plates. For a clean-looking finish, miter the wallpaper's corners.
- Cover picture mats with the same pattern of wallpaper you use for framing pictures.

FRAMING A PLATE WITH A WALLPAPER BORDER

HANDY HINTS

For easier removal, always cover the wall with wallpaper sizing before applying the wallpaper frames.

If an edge or corner of the wallpaper has not adhered to the wall after it dries, apply a small bit of white craft glue to the back of the paper, then press flat with a sponge.

1 Using a measuring tape, measure the circumference of the plate, then measure and cut a piece of wallpaper border the same length. Repeat for each plate you wish to display within a wallpaper frame.

2 Draw a horizontal line down the center of the wrong side of the wallpaper border, then draw vertical lines spaced 1 inch apart. Cut vertical lines on both sides of the wallpaper to within ⅛ inch of the center line.

3 With a small brush, apply water to the back of the border. Position border so inside edges are aligned with the pencil line and overlap to form a circle. The outside edges will have slight gaps between them.

OOPS

If the wallpaper frame tears into two pieces before it is applied to the walls, apply the first piece to the wall, then position the second piece next to the first, overlapping the inside edges and leaving a gap between outside edges.

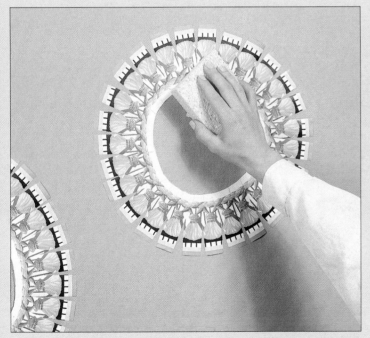

4 Continue applying the wallpaper border until the entire circle is formed. For pieces of the border that are not properly aligned, carefully lift the edge of the paper and reposition. With a damp sponge, smooth edges flat. Repeat for all plates.

CUSTOMIZED PHOTO RAILS

Decorative moldings transform a plain wall into an exciting photo gallery.

YOU WILL NEED
- ❏ 3-INCH-WIDE PICTURE FRAME MOLDING
- ❏ PHOTOGRAPHS
- ❏ PAINT & PAINTBRUSH
- ❏ #6 FINISHING NAILS
- ❏ HAMMER
- ❏ WOOD PUTTY & PUTTY KNIFE
- ❏ SANDPAPER
- ❏ PENCIL & SPIRIT LEVEL
- ❏ CLEAN CLOTH

BEFORE YOU BEGIN

Vary the height of a photo rail to ensure maximum visibility for photos. Try a chair rail for sitting rooms, a plate or ceiling rail for kitchens and bedrooms.

Working with Molding

Often added for architectural detail in a room, molding is generally made from soft woods such as pine or fir.
• Molding is available in frame shops, but is less expensive when purchased from a home supply center or lumberyard.
• Look for flat pieces free of knots and blemishes with straight, even edges.

Types of Wood Molding

Use a picture frame molding with an L-shaped groove cut along one inner edge. When in place, the photos will rest in the groove.

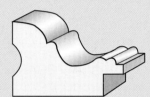

There are both formal and simple moldings with this indent (right). Choose one to fit the style of your decor.

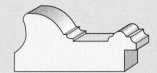

If you prefer a rounded or flat molding without the groove, glue a ⅛-inch-wide strip of wood to the back to hold it away from the wall and create a support for photos.

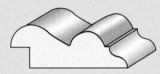

Finishing Molding

Wooden molding is usually sold unfinished.

For best results, paint the molding before attaching it to the wall. Use an easy-to-clean, enamel-based paint.

Begin by applying primer. Let dry, then apply a second coat to hide the grain of the wood, if necessary. Finish with two coats of paint.

Nail the molding in place, then touch up the nail holes.

If you decide to mount another photo rail to an adjacent wall, miter the corners of the molding to ensure an exact fit.

CREATING A PHOTO RAIL

HANDY HINTS

If desired, press a piece of double-sided tape on the back of each photo before placing it inside the photo rail. This temporarily secures the photo until you remove it from the wall.

1 Using a spirit level, measure and mark top placement line for molding. Below first line, draw a second placement line at eye level—considering height of photographs you wish to display along rail.

2 Turn top piece of molding so L-shaped groove is facing down and run a bead of glue across back. Line up lower edge with top pencil line. Using a hammer, nail molding in place every 6 inches with finishing nails.

3 Repeat gluing for second piece of molding. With L-shaped groove facing up, align molding with bottom placement line and again nail in place every 6 inches. If needed, countersink nails with a nailset.

4 With a putty knife, cover nail holes on molding with putty; let dry. Lightly sand putty spots with sandpaper. Wipe away any dust with a clean cloth, then touch up molding with matching paint.

5 Once paint has dried, begin placing photographs into photo rail. If desired, predetermine placement of photographs by laying them on floor against wall. To place photos into display rail, carefully bend top and bottom edges toward back of photograph and slip them between moldings.

ONE-OF-A-KIND WALL TREATMENTS

Personalize a room with favorite bits of collected memorabilia.

BEFORE YOU BEGIN

Hiding in a drawer or gathering dust in an unused closet is bound to be a memory-packed collection that would prove perfect for decorating walls.

Choosing Decorations

A postcard collection holds enormous potential for wall decorations, whether it includes postcards collected on travels through the years, "wish-you-were-here" messages from friends or old-fashioned Victorian treasures.

Seed packets make pretty wall decorations for a pantry or kitchen. Cut the front panel from the back to paste the cover flat to the wall.

Consider old sheet music or songbook pages as noteworthy wallcoverings for a music room or even a library. As an alternative, mount the pages without a break or space in between.

Children's artwork, from a single developmental period or gathered through the years, could decorate a hallway, student's study or grandparent's room.

Old photos feature wonderful subject matter, but photocopy them first and preserve the original.

Devote a wall to a specific, favorite decade and choose vintage magazine pages that depict cultural highlights or historic milestones.

Consider envelopes from international pen pals, complete with attractive foreign stamps.

On Display

A few guidelines for an attractive display:
• In general, items that are grouped closely together will emphasize an overall pattern; items placed with space between them will call greater attention to each individual picture.
• The similarity or difference in the sizes and shapes of the items will have an effect on the overall display.

DECORATING A WALL WITH POSTCARDS

HANDY HINTS

For an added touch, paint a border around each card to serve as a free-form "frame" for the gallery.

Paper cards usually soak up the first layer of polyurethane. After the second coat, observe the work to see if the wall looks smooth and evenly glossy. If not, apply another coat. Damp, steamy rooms such as bathrooms usually require three coats for optimum protection.

1 Use painter's masking tape to position postcards on the wall. Experiment with the spacing, standing back to view the effect; place favorite cards in the most visible spots. Mark the placement of finalized positions.

2 Holding the postcard against a piece of cardboard to guard against overspray, coat the back of the postcard with repositionable spray-mount adhesive. Spray in a crosshatch pattern to cover the card completely.

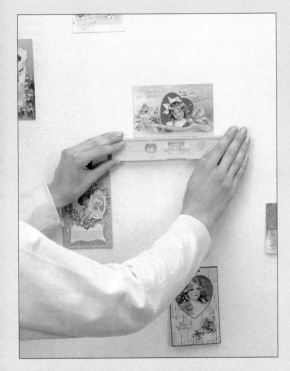

3 Affix the card to the wall at the desired spot. Check the position with a small spirit level to make sure it is even; reposition if necessary. Repeat the procedure with the remaining postcards.

4 After all the cards are affixed to the wall, brush two or three coats of polyurethane over the entire wall with a disposable foam brush. Allow the polyurethane to dry thoroughly between coats.

Recessed Shelving for Storage and Display

Pretty recessed niches add stylish storage space to your home.

YOU WILL NEED

❏ 1- BY 4-INCH, 1- BY 3-INCH & 1- BY 2-INCH WOOD BOARDS
❏ SCRAP OF 2- BY 4-INCH WOOD
❏ ½-INCH-THICK BIRCH PLYWOOD
❏ WOOD GLUE
❏ HAMMER & NAILS
❏ PRIMER & PAINT
❏ SPONGE BRUSH
❏ SANDPAPER
❏ CABINET KNOBS
❏ PUTTY & PUTTY KNIFE

BEFORE YOU BEGIN

The finished size of this shelf is 12 by 46 inches. Each box measures 12 by 14 inches.

Niche Notes

Using wall studs as a guide, draw shelf placement as desired on the wall; cut out with a sheetrock knife.

Cut the following:
- six pieces 1- by 4-inch boards, 14 inches long
- six pieces 1 by 4, 11 inches long
- three pieces 1 by 4, 13 inches long
- two pieces 1 by 3, 11 inches long
- two pieces 1 by 2, 11 inches long
- two pieces 1 by 2, 48 inches long
- three 12- by 14-inch pieces of birch to assemble the recessed frame and its boxes.

From ½-inch-thick pine, cut:
- four $6\frac{3}{8}$- by 5-inch pieces
- four $2\frac{1}{4}$- by 5-inch pieces
- two $2\frac{1}{4}$- by $5\frac{3}{8}$-inch pieces for drawers.

Painting Preparation

Begin by preparing the surface for painting. Wipe clean with a soft rag; sand with a fine-grade sandpaper. Wipe away the dust. Repeat process, if necessary.

When applying masking tape, be sure to press the edges flat with your finger to prevent the stain from seeping under.

Use only gel stains—they are easier to control since regular stains will seep more easily under the masking tape. Gel stains are available in a variety of colors including metallics and decorator colors, as well as wood tones. They are easily found at hardware and craft stores.

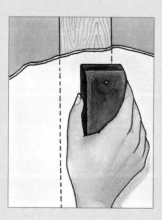

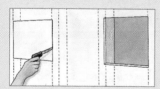

MAKING A RECESSED SHELF

1 For each box, align 11-inch pieces of wood along inside edges of 14-inch pieces; glue and nail in place. Slide 13-inch piece of 1- by 3-inch wood inside frame, center, then glue and nail in place.

2 Position 12- by 14-inch piece of birch on back of each box. Glue together with wood glue, then nail in place along edges. Be sure to wipe excess glue from inside and back of boxes.

3 Place 2- by 4-inch piece of wood between boxes as a spacer, leaving ⅛-inch space on each side. Center 11-inch piece of 1 by 3 over sides of each box and nail in place. Repeat for remaining box.

5 For each drawer, align 2¼-inch by 5-inch pieces of ½-inch-thick birch along inside edges of 6⅜-inch by 5-inch pieces; glue and nail in place. Wipe away any excess glue and ensure outside edges of wood pieces are aligned.

4 For frame sides, center 11-inch pieces of 1- by 2-inch wood over side edges of shelf. Align inside edges; glue and nail in place. Repeat for top and bottom of frame using 48-inch pieces of wood.

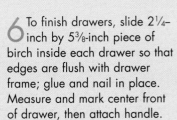

6 To finish drawers, slide 2¼–inch by 5⅜-inch piece of birch inside each drawer so that edges are flush with drawer frame; glue and nail in place. Measure and mark center front of drawer, then attach handle.

7 Place shelf inside wall opening so that frame covers exposed wood in wall. Nail shelf in place along wall stud using #8 nails. Putty nail holes and touch up with paint.

MAKEOVERS FOR BRICK WALLS

A cool coat of color redefines style while maintaining textural interest.

YOU WILL NEED

❏ MASONRY PRIMER
❏ PAINT ROLLERS
❏ LATEX PAINT
❏ MASKING TAPE
❏ DRILL & MASONRY BIT
❏ PLASTIC WALL ANCHORS
❏ 2½-INCH #6 SCREWS
❏ HAMMER

BEFORE YOU BEGIN

Before transforming your brick walls, take some time to clean and prepare them—this extra attention ensures longer lasting good looks.

Prepping and Cleaning the Wall

To guarantee proper paint adhesion, repair the wall and clean it thoroughly. Sweep the entire surface with a stiff-bristle or wire brush to remove loose dust or crumbled mortar (below).

Check for mortar that is in poor condition. If there are large cracks or missing chunks, use a chisel to clean and deepen the area. Fill the gap with mortar or latex patching cement and smooth it; let dry completely.

Mix a cleaning solution of muriatic acid diluted in water (a ½ pint of acid per gallon of water). This will dissolve any dusty calcified salts from the mortar as well as built-up grease, dirt and oil. Brush it carefully onto the bricks with a stiff brush, making certain to protect yourself and your clothing.

Rinse or spray the wall with water. Allow it to dry overnight before painting.

Design Options

• Enhance textural interest by sponge painting the primed bricks.
• Even if the room lacks a fireplace, put up a mantel shelf or fireplace surround to add character; paint a stylized fire in the hearth for whimsical appeal.
• Accent random bricks or create a defined pattern with a few colors that contrast the base color.

• Stencil a border for a chair rail or choose an all-over pattern, using the bricks' mortar as ready-made guidelines for the motifs. Or stamp on a design with a shape cut from a sponge.
• Give a basement the illusion of being an upstairs room by painting "windows" with scenic views on the bricks.

DECORATING A BRICK WALL

1 Coat the prepared brick wall (Before You Begin) with a stain-killing primer. Use a roller cover with long fibers to ensure even coverage in all the nooks and crannies. Repeat coats of primer as necessary; let dry.

2 After the primer has had sufficient drying time, roll a topcoat of latex paint over the primed wall, again using a clean, long-fibered roller cover. Allow to dry thoroughly and apply a second coat, if desired.

3 Decide upon placement of the mirrors or other wall art and mark the spot for the hook with an "X" of masking tape. Make sure to position the "X" over one of the mortar joints rather than the brick.

HANDY HINTS

Drill into masonry slowly to prevent the tool from overheating. Always unplug the drill before changing bits.

TAKE NOTE

Read the warning label and handle muriatic acid carefully—it's odorous and toxic: use adequate ventilation; wear goggles, gloves and long sleeves to protect your eyes, hands and arms; keep children away from work in progress.

4 Mark the exact center of each masking-tape "X" with a nail or nail punch to create a starting guide. Using a drill fitted with a 3/16-inch masonry bit, drill a 1½-inch-deep hole at the center of each "X" marked.

5 Insert a ¼-inch plastic anchor into each drilled hole and tap it in place gently with a hammer. Using a hand-held screwdriver, slowly insert a #6 screw into each hole. Leave a small amount of the screw protruding.

6 Hang the mirror or other artwork onto the protruding screw, making sure it is secure. Adjust the mirror as necessary; check the position with a level to make sure the mirror hangs evenly.

Wood Paneling Makeovers

Creative painting turns ordinary paneling into a stunning backdrop.

BEFORE YOU BEGIN

Taking time to prepare the paneled surface for painting will save time and effort during the project, and will ensure that the paint finish is applied correctly.

Preparing the Paneling

Washing paneled walls removes grime and grit from the surface, allowing the paint to adhere directly to the paneling.

Wash the walls with a mixture of cleanser and water (below), or use a sponge mop to apply the solution. Rinse the sponge frequently for a cleaner surface.

Make sure the sponge is not saturated with cleaning solution. Otherwise, the walls will become damp and time will be needed to allow for thorough drying.

For laminate paneling with an oil finish, painting the paneling with latex paint will create a crackled finish because of the reaction between oil-based and water-based products.

For natural wood paneling, apply an oil-based primer to seal the wood and hide wood grain.

When applying a second coat, make sure nail holes, grain and grooves are thoroughly covered.

Trim Care

Carefully covering trimwork with masking tape (below) will prevent paint from damaging the finish.
• Purchase painter's masking tape. It adheres securely to the trim, but is easily removed without peeling off the paint underneath it.
• Apply tape so it is even with edges of trimwork. Overlap edges of tape pieces so trim is not exposed.

CRACKLE PAINTING OVER PANELING

1 Using the side of the paint-brush, paint a base coat of latex paint into the grooves of the paneling where a roller can't reach. Then, use the brush to cut in the edges of the base-board, ceiling and corners.

2 Using a roller, paint the pan-eling with the base coat of latex paint. Don't worry about covering the wall completely. The oily surface of the paneling will give the paint a crackled appearance. Let dry.

3 Wash the paint roller, being careful to clean off all old paint. Then lightly apply a sec-ond color of latex paint over the base coat. For contrast, be sure that the base coat is still visible in places. Allow to dry.

HANDY HINTS

When layering colors, begin painting with an accent color, the color you want to be the least visible, and end with the color you want to dominate the wall.

TAKE NOTE

Latex paints are easy to clean with soap and water, and are fast drying. They give a clear, graphic pattern.

Oil-based or alkyd paints have a slower drying time, but are more durable than latex finishes. This finish is usually soft and muted.

4 Dip a large natural sponge into a light-colored top coat of paint. Dab the sponge on a piece of paper or plastic to remove excess paint, then begin lightly sponging the wall. Work from one side to the other to ensure that the sponging finish is even. Let dry.

DECORATIVE TREATMENTS FOR PANELED DOORS

Turn plain, paneled doors into something special with wallpaper, stencils and paint.

YOU WILL NEED

- ❑ ANAGLYPTA WALLPAPER
- ❑ LATEX PAINTS
- ❑ PAINTBRUSH
- ❑ WALLPAPER ADHESIVE
- ❑ RUBBER ROLLER
- ❑ CRAFT KNIFE
- ❑ T SQUARE RULE
- ❑ RAZOR BLADE

BEFORE YOU BEGIN

Decorating a door is an inexpensive renovating technique that can disguise cosmetic flaws on an existing door.

Prepare Door

Clean the door and sand it smooth, then remove sanding dust with a cloth.

Remove strips of molding from the inside of panels and paint in a matching or contrasting color.

If painting the door, take off the doorknob and paint the door with semigloss.

Panel Designs

Panel designs can also be applied with a stencil (below left). Or, sponge paint a simple motif like a checkerboard design (below right). Repeat the design in all the panels for continuity. Apply a clear coat of polyurethane to protect the finished design.

DECORATING A DOOR

HANDY HINTS

Add wallpaper sizing to the door panels before applying wallpaper. This makes it easier to remove the paper at a later date.

The wallpaper may shrink or stretch a little when rolled with adhesive, so allow for extra room when measuring and cutting it to fit the door panels.

1 Measure door panels, adding 1 inch to one side and bottom to allow for adjustments. Lay out wallpaper on clean surface. With design centered, measure wallpaper. Cut out wallpaper using T square and craft knife.

2 Lay wallpaper piece face-down on newspaper. Using 3-inch rubber roller, apply wallpaper adhesive evenly to back of wallpaper, completely covering surface. Repeat with remaining pieces.

3 To allow adhesive to spread evenly on back of wallpaper, fold each wallpaper piece in half with adhesive sides together, being careful not to crease fold; let sit for four minutes. This process is called *booking*.

QUICK FIX

Small tears in the wallpaper will fade away once the paper is applied to the door panel. Apply wallpaper to the door with adhesive, carefully smoothing the torn area in place with a damp sponge; let dry.

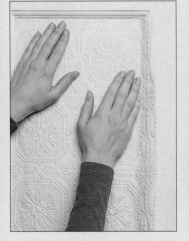

4 Unfold wallpaper, align top left corner of wallpaper with top left corner of door panel; press corner flat with fingers. Working from corner, smooth paper to door panel with hands to remove any air pockets.

5 Press paper firmly along right side and bottom edge, forming crease in excess paper. Using craft knife, cut excess wallpaper even with panel. Using damp sponge, remove excess adhesive on all surfaces.

6 Allow wallpaper to dry completely. Using semigloss paint, apply light base coat on wallpaper; let dry. If color is different from door, tape over molding with low adhesive painter's tape for protection.

7 Using almost-dry brush, apply darker topcoat of paint over base coat to emphasize relief design of wallpaper. Remove painter's tape from molding. Use razor blade to remove any paint mistakes from molding, if necessary.

LIKE-NEW VINYL FLOORS

Revitalize worn vinyl floors with contemporary painted designs.

BEFORE YOU BEGIN

Paint is an inexpensive alternative to removing and replacing vinyl floors. Choose a quality paint, keep designs to a minimum in heavy traffic areas and apply several coats of polyurethane to extend the floor's life.

Pointers for Painting Floors

Vinyl that is worn, dull and smooth works best for this project. For shiny vinyls, sand to remove the sheen. Avoid painting floors with holes and dents.

Clean the floor to remove dirt and wax buildup.

Use a liquid deglosser on both dulled and sanded vinyl floors to improve the bonding ability of the paint. Apply painter's masking tape around cabinets and walls, then begin by cutting in the edges of the floor and hard-to-reach areas with a paintbrush.

Painting Styles

While the floor's tile line or pattern may show through when painted, it can be disguised or highlighted with certain techniques. Choose a style that will work with your floor.

Create a speckled stone finish by spattering three to five coordinating colors over the base coats. Thin each paint and lightly tap the brush for the desired effect.

Or, paint a checkerboard design over the base coat. Once the paint is dry, gently sand until flecks of the first coat appear.

Template Tips

• Enlarge the template (below) to the desired size and cut out with scissors.
• If creating your own template, look for large designs that will be visible and effective on the floor.

• Keep in mind that designs with intricate edges are more difficult to paint, while geometric designs can be transferred to the floor with ease.

PAINTING OVER VINYL FLOORS

1 Transfer the template (Before You Begin) to a piece of cardboard. Using a craft knife, cut out the template. Keep the template edges as smooth as possible to make transferring the template to the vinyl easier.

2 Using a paint roller, apply a base coat of paint over the vinyl. Apply as many coats of paint as needed to cover the preprinted colors on the vinyl. Be sure to allow the paint to dry thoroughly between each coat.

3 Beginning along one wall and working toward the center, create a grid on the floor by dividing it into 18-inch squares (or pick a size that divides it evenly). Use a colored chalk line to mark the placement of the squares.

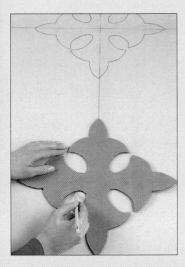

5 Paint the template using a paintbrush and a darker color of paint, covering the pencil outline. Let dry, then add another coat, if necessary. Seal the entire floor with several coats of non-yellowing polyurethane.

4 Beginning in the middle of the floor, position the center of the template at the intersection of four squares. Line up the template's points with the lines drawn on the floor and trace the template with a pencil.

STENCILED TILES

Paint a pattern onto existing wall tiles to update and brighten a room.

YOU WILL NEED
❑ STENCIL CARD
❑ STENCIL BRUSH
❑ ARTIST'S ACRYLIC PAINTS
❑ ACRYLIC VARNISH
❑ CRAFT KNIFE
❑ MASKING TAPE
❑ DETERGENT
❑ PENCIL & PAPER
❑ STICKY LABELS

BEFORE YOU BEGIN

Stenciling on tile is easy and effective. Use precut stencils (found at a craft or paint store) that have simple motifs, or create your own using this template as an easy guide.

Preparing Stencils and Tiles

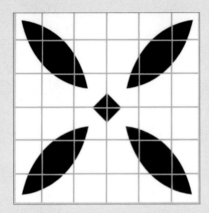

This motif (above) is 2-inch square. To enlarge it on a copier, select 200% for 4-inch tiles. Take that version and enlarge that by 150% for 6-inch tiles. If you do not have access to a copier, follow the next step.

Measure a 4- or 6-inch square (to match tile size) onto paper and divide it into a grid of 36 equal squares (for 4 inch, they will be ⅔ inch and for 6 inch, they will be 1-inch square). Copy the design from the motif (below).

Stick drawing or copy to clear acetate or waxed stencil card. Cut out design through both template and stencil card (below) using a sharp craft knife. Then cut around the edge so stencil is exactly 4- or 6-inch square.

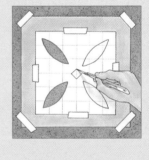

• Wipe tiled areas with an abrasive grease-removing detergent to create a clean surface for paint to adhere to.
• Tape a piece of paper to the wall and practice the technique to get used to loading the brush and stenciling correctly for an upright position—that is, without drips.
• Plan where the motifs will go. Mark those tiles with sticky labels which can be peeled off as you work.

STENCILING WALL TILES

1 Place your stencil over the tile so that the design is centered and the edges follow the grout lines. The waxed side should be facing out so paint will wipe off. Secure firmly in place with masking tape.

2 Dip brush into paint and blot excess onto a cloth so brush is almost dry. Hold cut edges of stencil design flat against tile to prevent seepage and apply paint sparingly, either as flat color or graduated tones.

3 After 5 minutes, remove the stencil and check motif for any imperfect edges. Gently scrape off unwanted marks with a craft knife, but be careful—the stenciled motif is not completely dry and is easy to scratch.

HANDY HINTS

Use a varnish that matches the tile. Put gloss varnish on gloss tiles, and satin or matte varnish on matte tiles.

TAKE NOTE

Wipe excess paint from stencil card after each use to avoid transferring marks to new tile. If using more than one color, cut separate stencils for each one.

4 When you have finished stenciling, allow paint to dry thoroughly (at least two hours). Dust tiles lightly to remove any scrapings that may be left from using the craft knife. Seal with a coat of acrylic varnish, applied with vertical strokes.

CREATIVE WALLPAPER BORDERS

Put your creative stamp on a room with a custom-made border.

YOU WILL NEED

- ❏ WALLPAPER ROLL
- ❏ WALLPAPER PASTE
- ❏ SPIRIT LEVEL
- ❏ CRAFT KNIFE
- ❏ SMOOTHING BRUSH
- ❏ SEAM ROLLER
- ❏ BROAD KNIFE
- ❏ STRAIGHTEDGE
- ❏ MEASURING TAPE
- ❏ SPONGE

BEFORE YOU BEGIN

All you need is a sharp-edged craft knife and some leftover wallpaper to create a wallpaper border. A spirit level also helps you make sure the line is true.

Measuring Border Areas

Measure all wall areas that will have a border and combine for a subtotal. Then add any of the following figures that apply to get the total amount needed.
- Allow extra for pattern repeats if matching patterns at the corners.

- Add 2 inches for each edge that will be mitered.
- If a wall, door or other trim area is a focal point, start the project by centering the border there. Work out from that point to keep the best part exactly where you want it.

Mitering Corners

Paste down the first border strip, making sure the border extends several inches beyond the corner where it will be mitered. Position the second strip at a right angle (below), overlapping the border strips so the pattern motifs of both strips lie on top of each other. Paste the second strip into place and smooth out.

To miter, place a ruler or straightedge from inner to outer corners of overlapping borders. Cut through both border strips at the same time with a craft knife (below). Remove the excess cut paper ends so corner halves join together at a right angle. Press wallpaper edges down with a seam roller.

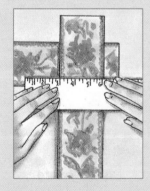

CUTTING BORDERS FROM WALLPAPER

1 Cut wallpaper carefully with a craft knife and a straight-edge. Pressing the knife against the straightedge helps to cut a straight line and avoids cutting into design. Cut as many strips as possible at this time.

2 Using a spirit level, mark a light pencil line around the room at the desired height to provide a guideline for border placement. Paste and book first border strip according to the manufacturer's directions.

3 Hang border paper. Brush paper to get rid of air bubbles and make sure paste will adhere uniformly to wall. Use seam roller to press down edges. Wipe off the excess paste with a damp sponge.

TAKE NOTE

Work with a partner who will hold the pasted, booked border while you position and apply the wallpaper. The work will go easy and fast.

OOPS

If you cut into the pattern, all is not lost. Just be careful when pasting the paper—the cut edges will lie flat and unnoticeable once up on the wall and smoothed down.

4 For seams that fall in the middle of walls, overlap border strips to match patterns. Then cut through both layers with craft knife. Use broad knife or straightedge as cutting guide.

5 Peel back the border and remove the cut ends. Be sure the pattern meets. Press the wallpaper flat. Miter the edges at the corners for a professional look. Refer to Before You Begin for instructions on mitering. Make sure to wipe any excess paste from the wallpaper and wall. Continue applying border strips as described in Steps 1-4.

PAINTED SISAL RUG

Enhance a sisal rug by highlighting the weave with shades of paint.

BEFORE YOU BEGIN

A sisal rug made up of squares is the easiest to use when creating a design. Simply count the squares, plot the count on graph paper and design a pattern. Then use the graph paper pattern as a guide when painting.

Planning the Design

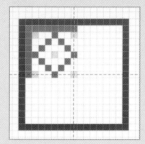

Use colored pencils to fill in design and make the pattern easy to follow when painting.

Practice on a small strip of sisal to determine the intensity of the colors and see how they look against the natural color of the sisal rug.

Follow the rug weave to create a paint-within-the-lines design that eliminates masking edges. Count the number of rug squares across and down on graph paper (above), divide into quadrants and work out a pattern that fits.

This design is 8½ feet by 8½ feet if each rug square is 6 inches. On a 9- by 9-foot rug, cut off one row of squares on length and width. Then tie the thread ends to keep them from unraveling.

Graph the entire design (right) to make sure that the pattern works out evenly to the size of the rug and to see how the finished design will look. Any extra space can be made part of the border.

Painting Tips

• Stores that sell sisal by the yard can cut a one-yard piece for practice.
• The color will be deeper and darker if the paint is not wiped off after application. When wiped, the lighter, soaked-in look lets the natural qualities of the sisal show.
• Work on the floor—it's the largest flat surface around. Place a tarp on the floor beneath the sisal to protect from spills.

PAINTING THE PATTERN

1 Work with one color at a time. When painting a pattern, use colored stickers to mark placement of each paint color. These stickers are available at office supply and stationery stores.

2 Mix half paint and half water into a small bucket. Blend thoroughly. Put a lot of paint onto the brush as you work; the rug will absorb it. Brush paint onto surface, working one square at a time.

3 Wipe off excess paint with a paper towel to get a variegated look. This also removes some of the paint to prevent cracking or chipping later on. The paint dries quickly, so wipe after 1 or 2 squares.

HANDY HINTS

Rest one arm over the other arm while working to keep the painting arm steady. This extra support helps keep painting lines straight.

DOLLAR SENSE

A pint of paint goes a long way on this project because it is thinned with an equal amount of water. Mix small quantities at a time.

OOPS

If you paint a square the wrong color or spill paint, let the paint set until it's dry. Then peel off the layer of paint with your fingernail.

4 Paint all designated squares with the second color. Continue with one color at a time until the pattern is complete. When rug is finished, save any remaining paint for touch-ups if heavily traveled areas begin to show wear.

BEAUTIFUL RAGGED WALLS

Brighten up plain walls with this quick and easy paint effect.

BEFORE YOU BEGIN

Ragging off a top glaze of paint color reveals some of the paint underneath. This gives walls a dappled finish, which is easier on the eye than flat color.

Using Colorless Glaze

Glaze dilutes paint and makes it translucent and easier to work with. Water-based glazes dry very quickly, so colorless oil-based glaze is used for ragging to allow more time to dab off the glaze and create the pattern.

• The proportion of glaze to add to paint depends on the desired depth of color desired.

• The more paint added, the stronger and deeper the color becomes.

• For this reason, introduce the paint gradually and mix each stage well until the right depth of color is achieved.

• Choose a tint glaze shade that coordinates with other colors and shades in the room.

The Results in Detail

For ragging off, the glaze is applied over an opaque base coat and lifted off with dabs from a scrunched rag (below top).

Rag rolling also lifts the glaze to reveal the base coat underneath, but cloth is twisted and then rolled, not dabbed (below bottom).

RAGGING WALLS

HANDY HINTS

Any type of cloth can be used, and each will produce a slightly different effect depending on the pattern of the weave. Cloths must be clean and free from dust because fluff in the fabric is likely to end up on the walls.

1 To prepare the walls, wash them down and fill any cracks. Apply a base coat of eggshell finish paint. Let dry overnight, then apply a second coat if necessary for an even finish. Let dry.

2 Use artist's oil paint (not acrylic) to give the glaze its color. Start by squeezing about an inch of the paint into a bowl and dilute it with a splash of mineral spirits. Stir well to blend completely.

3 Mix the paint with ready-made glaze in a bucket. Check instructions on glaze can for coverage. Pour required amount of glaze into bucket. Add a little diluted paint. Stir thoroughly and test for color.

TAKE NOTE

When ragging, work quickly so that a section is completed before the glaze dries. This is known as keeping a wet edge. The second section worked will only blend with the first while the glaze is still wet. For this reason, choose simple and small projects to start with—like a fireplace column or striped wall panel.

4 When the color of the glaze is just right, pour it into a roller tray and apply to the wall. Only cover about a square yard at a time or the glaze will dry before the ragging work has been finished.

5 Tear up an old sheet or a similar clean, lint-free cloth into 18-inch squares. Scrunch one up. Keep the others handy—cloths will need to be replaced as they become saturated with the glaze.

6 Start at one corner of the area of wet glaze and dab the scrunched rag swiftly over it, removing some of the color to let the base show through. Paint the next area of glaze and repeat, blending sections neatly.

DOOR PANELS WITH MOLDING

Define a plain door by gluing on molding to add a new dimension.

YOU WILL NEED

❏ HOLLOW CORE DOOR
❏ DECORATIVE MOLDING
❏ MITER BOX & SAW
❏ LATEX PAINT
❏ PAINTBRUSH
❏ GLUE GUN & GLUE
   STICKS
❏ WOOD GLUE
❏ MEASURING TAPE

BEFORE YOU BEGIN

Whether detailed or plain, straight or curved, moldings can define a bare, hollow core door and give it the appearance of an older, more substantial one. Choose a design and color treatment that complement the room the door opens into.

Creating a Panel by Design

Decide on panel shapes by practicing on scrap paper. The panel dimensions should complement the scale of the door and adjoining panels.

Straight lengths of molding are available from 6 feet to 16 feet at lumberyards and some hardware stores. Add

dimensions for panels plus extra for mitering.

Or look for molding kits that have cut lengths of molding with the edges already mitered. Some include shaped molding pieces for a panel with a curved top.

Detailed molding for formality

Paint a light color for emphasis

Color Choices

• Whether the wood is painted or stained, coordinate the colors with the room's décor.
• Create a dramatic contrast by painting the door a dark

color and the molding panels and trim a light color.
• Or stain the molding and trim a slightly darker shade for a shadow effect in either a casual or formal room.

PLACING THE DOOR MOLDING

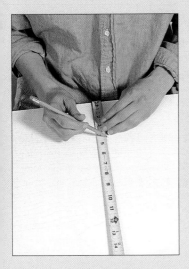

1 Remove door from hinges and place on flat, protected surface. Prepare door: repair nicks, sand and paint. Determine panel sizes. Measure and mark these dimensions on the door, checking position with a level.

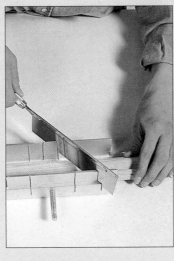

2 Measure lengths of molding and mark at the top edge with a pencil. Determine angle of cut for mitered corner. Use miter box to cut the molding edge. Sand any rough spots on cut edge.

3 When all the molding edges have been cut for one panel, arrange them in the desired shape. Make sure all corners fit snugly. Sand or re-cut the edges that do not join together smoothly.

HANDY HINTS

Secure narrow moldings in the miter box by adding a wood scrap to fill the space. Look for small miter boxes with adjustable holding screws in hardware stores.

TAKE NOTE

If you're using a decorative molding, keep the decorative edge to the outside when determining the miter angle to cut.

4 Paint the surfaces of the molding pieces. Let dry completely. Apply a zigzag row of wood glue to the underside of the molding. When wood glue dries, it is strong enough to hold molding to door without nails.

5 Just before positioning on the door, add dots of hot glue to molding ends and place on marked lines. Hot glue sets quickly and holds molding in place until wood glue dries. Work from the top down.

Colorwashed Texture for Walls

Add depth and texture to walls with simple brushing and blending.

BEFORE YOU BEGIN

Colorwashing imparts a rich, warm glow to walls and ceilings. However, the choice of colors and the way they are applied can make a big difference in the final effect you achieve.

Use of Color

The combinations of colors used for colorwashing can produce different results.
• The thinner the glaze, the better the effect.
• A lighter glaze applied over a darker one will produce an aged effect.
• Warm colors give rooms a glowing, sunshiny look.
• Pale blues and greens can look almost luminous.

• Either use various shades of the same color for a subtle effect or combine different, but related, colors for drama.
• Pale colors over a pale base often look more casual than darker colors.
• Dark colors over a pale base look different than using pale colors over a dark base; experiment.

Colorwashing Effects

Two shades of a violet-blue glaze applied over a darker shade of the same color produce the airy feel of a cloudless summer sky. Ensuring that the brush strokes are carefully blended leaves the wall looking softly dappled and soothing.

A combination of three different, but related, colors results in a dramatic effect that is nonetheless harmonious. Using the sponge in more of a dabbing than blending motion gives the wall a textured look that seems to produce a feeling of movement.

COLORWASHING A WALL

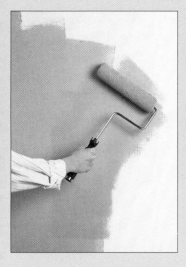

1 Before painting, ensure wall is clean and dry. Patch any holes with putty; sand smooth. Use roller to apply base coat. For added texture, apply paint with a high-nap roller. Roll strokes in varying directions.

2 While waiting for base coat to dry, prepare paint for second coat. In plastic bucket, dilute darker paint with an equal quantity of cold water. Add pre-mixed glaze according to instructions on can; mix well.

3 Brush on glaze mixture in a random, crosshatch motion, leaving at least 50% of base coat exposed. Work on one small (4- by 4-foot) area of wall at a time, so paint won't dry before it's blended (Step 4).

4 Use damp, flat sponge to blend wet paint in a circular rubbing motion, varying direction and arc of motion. Repeat Steps 3 and 4 until all of base coat is covered with glaze. Be sure to blend overlapping areas well.

5 Dilute base paint as shown in Step 2. When wall paint is dry, sparingly brush more mixed color on top. Work on one small area at a time, blending strokes over completed areas. Work quickly so paint does not dry.

6 Use a damp sponge in a random motion to blend top coat and soften "hard" lines, producing a subtle, textured effect.

PATTERNED FLOORS

Turn a porch floor into the center of attention by staining it with color.

BEFORE YOU BEGIN

Plan the design carefully on graph paper before marking it on the floor, to ensure that the pattern and border will fit your room's dimensions.

Planning the Design

Plan the design on graph paper to determine box and border sizes. Lengthen the border and repeat box design to fill size of floor. On this diagram, each design element is labeled with a letter or number for easy color reference. Follow this key:

• Cream = Base
• Gray = 1, B, D
• Green = 1, A, C

Using Wood Stain

Stains are thinner than paints and let the wood grain show through the color. They are available in wood tones and colors.

When applying stain in patterns, it is essential to use masking tape to define the lines. Stain can seep under stencil templates.

Using a Chalk Line

A chalk line (or snapline) makes it easy to mark long, straight lines on flat surfaces such as floors and walls.
• A chalk line consists of a 50- to 100-foot string coiled inside a container of powdered chalk.

• To use, simply unreel the string and hold it taut over the area to be marked. Snap the string and a line of chalk will drop onto the surface.
• Chalk lines are available at hardware stores.

STAINING THE PATTERN ON THE FLOOR

1 Using a paintbrush, stain entire floor with base color; wipe off excess stain with clean cloth. Work on one small area at a time, brushing on and wiping off before stain dries.

2 Use T square and chalk line to mark border design. Outline squares labeled "1" with masking tape; place tape along outer edge of line. Stain squares green; wipe with clean cloth.

3 Remove tape from around squares. Tape off triangles labeled "2"; place outer edge of tape along inner edge of diamond shape and outside edge of shape "2". Apply gray stain; wipe off.

4 Use T square and chalk line to mark horizontal and vertical lines in center design. Mask along outside edge of entire design and outside all lines forming rectangles labeled "A".

5 Use a paintbrush to apply green stain to all As; wipe with clean cloth. Let stain dry completely before removing masking tape from only the short ends of all As.

6 Place masking tape along other side of chalk lines to mark out areas labeled "B". Apply gray stain to all Bs; wipe with clean cloth. Let stain dry completely.

7 Use a razor blade to cut tape away from short ends of areas labeled "C". Replace tape on other side of chalk lines. Apply green stain to all Cs; wipe off.

8 Use masking tape to outline diamonds labeled "D". Check measurements to ensure all diamonds are centered. Apply gray stain to all Ds; wipe off excess stain with clean cloth. When stain is dry, remove all masking tape. Seal entire floor with several coats of polyurethane to protect the design; sand lightly between each coat.

Vinyl Floor Tile Patterns

Create a unique and colorful work of art with flooring tiles.

YOU WILL NEED

☐ VINYL FLOORING TILES
☐ ADHESIVE
☐ SPREADING TROWEL
☐ UTILITY KNIFE & BLADES
☐ METAL STRAIGHTEDGE
☐ WOOD BOARD
☐ HAMMER
☐ LARGE SPONGE
☐ SOAP & WATER

BEFORE YOU BEGIN

For guaranteed success, make sure all the puzzle pieces will fit before you apply the adhesive. Plan design, colors and size on graph paper before taking a trip to the store.

Design Your Pattern

Using graph paper, map out the size and shape of the room. Measure the size of the room and floor tile in inches, not feet. Divide the room by the measured dimension of the floor tile to determine how many tiles are needed. Draw the design with one square on the graph paper equal to one square floor tile.

Choose flooring of identical thickness and composition. This may be more difficult when combining sheeting and tiles in one design. Varying textures will add interest to the design.

Use the graph below to reproduce the design at left. Adapt it to fit into the dimensions of your room.

For the best dollar value, learn how many tiles are sold in a box and plan your design around this number. Many tile stores do not sell individual tiles.

For pattern design inspiration, look to quilting books or puzzle designs. Children's blocks make terrific tools for experimenting with shapes and layouts. Use colored pencils to visualize how colors will work together.

Consider laying out a portion of the design without adhesive to check measurements and see how the pattern works in the room.

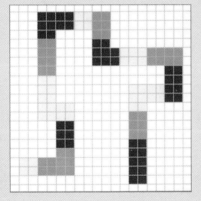

Preparation

Ask at the tile store about subflooring options for the type of tile you have.
• Always tile over a flat, clean surface with no cracks, recesses or protrusions.

• Do not apply new tiles over an existing floor. Remove the old floor.
• Raising the floor by adding a new layer of plywood is a bit more costly but sometimes a simpler solution than removing an old floor.

LAYING THE VINYL FLOORING

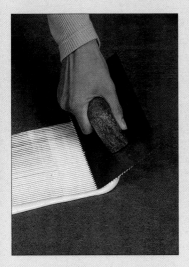

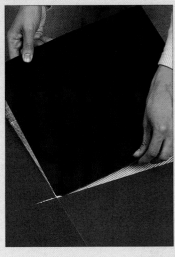

HANDY HINTS

Always allow the recommended drying time suggested by the manufacturer before walking on or returning furniture to the floor. Be especially generous with drying time if the weather is humid.

1 Beginning in the corner of the room farthest from your exit, pour adhesive on a section of floor only as far as your can comfortably reach—about 2 feet. Use the spreading trowel to evenly distribute the adhesive.

2 Starting at corner, lay first tile, two adjacent to it, and so on until prepared floor area is covered. Make sure all tiles fit firmly without spaces. Repeat with more adhesive and continue laying tiles.

3 Measure and mark tiles that need cutting. Working over wood board or old flooring, use utility knife and straightedge to score tile; do not cut through. Lay tile over table edge, and snap in two at scored line.

4 To mimic big rollers used by professional tilers, use a wood board to set tiles. Lift and move board; do not drag. Apply pressure to one section at a time until all tiles are set. Clean floor with soap and water or a recommended cleaning solution.

PAINTED DESIGNER STAIRS

Create a painted runner and add vibrant color to a stairway.

BEFORE YOU BEGIN

Measure and mark all the lines in advance, to make the job go quickly.

Preparation

• Refinish treads and handrail of banister, if necessary. Apply a fresh coat of paint to risers, sides of staircase and banister railings.

• Mark a line 5 inches in from sides of each stair.

• Apply masking tape along outer edges of both markings.

• Apply primer between tape to create a fake carpet runner and a foundation on which to decorate. Leave to dry.

• To create border lines, mark a line 5 inches in from each side of fake runner. Mark another line 1 inch in from first line; then again 1 inch from that.

Design Templates

PAINTING THE STAIRS

1 Apply 1½-inch-wide painter's masking tape to outer edges of other lines to create three 1-inch-wide unmasked strips along edges of "runner."

2 Draw lines between two inner tapes to divide depth of each tread and riser into three. Tape along bottom edges of lines. Use a craft knife to cut away top half of inner vertical tape line to form border design.

3 Apply yellow paint between outermost tape lines. Allow to dry completely. Apply a second coat of paint, if needed. When paint is dry, carefully remove all tape except strips along outer edges of border.

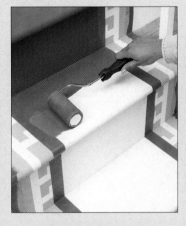

6 Use a photocopier to enlarge templates for central design (Before You Begin). Trace designs onto thin cardboard and cut out. Draw around paisley template on risers. Use second template to decorate landing.

4 Apply wide tape to inner edges of painted border. Use a roller and blue paint to cover center of runner. Allow paint to dry completely. Remove all tape except strips along outer edges of border.

5 Use a 1-inch-wide brush and blue paint to cover all areas showing white primer. To simplify process and protect yellow paint, mask long, straight, outer edges of border design with tape.

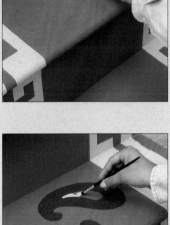

7 Use a thin brush to paint outside of paisley design red, and inside yellow. Repeat for second pattern on landing. Remove all remaining tape. Apply two or three coats of polyurethane to protect staircase. Allow to dry and sand lightly between coats.

PAINTED QUILT ON A WALL

Re-create the classic beauty of an Amish quilt with vibrant paint.

BEFORE YOU BEGIN

Measure the area that you want the quilt to fill, and then make a scale drawing of the quilt design on graph paper so that you can plan the dimensions in advance.

Planning the Quilt

Use the following dimensions to paint a 40- by 40-inch quilt to fit at the head of a double bed. The diagram shows the placement of the colors:

- Area 1 = 40 by 1 inch
- Area 2 = 30 by 4 inches
- Area 3 = 4 by 4 inches
- Area 4 = 22 by 4 inches
- Area 5 = 11 by 11 by 15.3 inches
- Area 6 = 2½ by 2½ inches
- Area 7 = 9.6 by 2.8 inches
- Area 8 = 9.6 by 9.6 inches

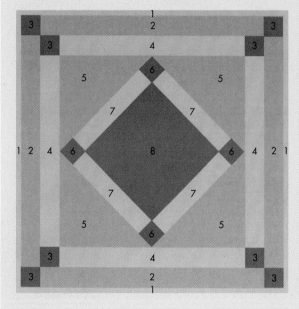

Choosing Designs and Colors

Traditional Amish quilts feature geometric designs, generally using a combination of diamonds, squares and triangles.

For an authentic look, choose a combination of dark and bright colors—purple, green and turquoise were popular Amish colors.

PAINTING THE QUILT

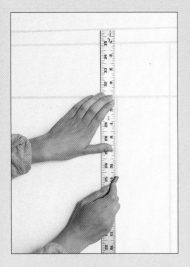

1 Use a T square and chalk to mark outline of quilt on wall. For very long lines, a chalk line can be used instead. Continue measuring and marking other lines for remainder of quilt (Before You Begin).

2 Outline all areas labeled "1" with painter's masking tape; place tape along outer edges of line. Outline inside edge of area labeled "2", again placing tape along outer edge of line.

3 Fill in area labeled "1" with green paint. When paint is dry, remove masking tape from around area 1. Tape off outer edge of area 2; place tape along outer edge of chalk line, partially covering area 1.

HANDY HINTS

A painted quilt looks best on a plain, neutral color wall. If the wall color is too dramatic, it will detract from the power of the quilt.

5 Fill in area 3 with red paint. When paint is dry, tape off area 4; fill in with green paint. When paint is dry, tape off area 5; fill in with purple paint. When paint is dry, tape off area 6; fill in with red paint. When paint is dry, tape off area 7; fill in with green paint. When paint is dry, tape off area 8; fill in with red paint. When taping off areas, always place tape along outer edges of area to be painted.

4 Fill in area 2 with purple paint. When paint is dry, remove masking tape from around area 2. Tape off area 3, placing tape along outer edge of lines.

Painted Quilt on a Wall 133

PAINTED SHOWER DOORS

Add a surprising touch of color with painted designs on glass.

BEFORE YOU BEGIN

Inspiration from nature transforms these ordinary shower doors into scenes from a summer garden. Painting the doors also adds privacy in bathrooms.

Prep Work for Painting Doors

Painting the doors will be easier if you take time to correctly position the pattern. It also helps to cover the metal frames with masking tape for protection.

• Pop shower doors from their tracks. With a soft pencil, mark the doors' top edges for reference.

• Using glass cleaner, clean the doors on both sides. Dry them thoroughly before starting.

• Cover the metal frames of the doors with masking tape. Press tape edges firmly to the metal to ensure a tight seal.

• Using a T square and pencil, find center of the doors and mark window placement (below). Measure the shingles, window frame and window box.

• Position tape on inside of placement line and press firmly to the glass; paint.

• When paint dries, replace the doors on their tracks.

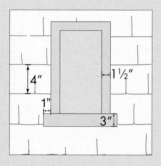

Template Tips

Randomly paint the leaves and flowers onto the glass for a natural finish.

• Allow the windows and shingles to dry before painting the motifs on the glass.

• Enlarge and transfer the templates (below) to heavy construction paper and cut them out with a craft knife or sharp scissors.

• Oil paints work best as they are less likely to scratch or flake.

• Use the decor in your bath as a color cue for painting the flowers.

PAINTING A SHOWER DOOR

1 Using a small paint roller, paint the shower doors with two coats of enamel paint. Roll the paint roller over the edges of the tape for straight lines. Let the paint dry one day between coats and one day after the last coat.

2 With a soft lead pencil, draw the window box and the molding around the window. To create the shingles, use a T square to make horizontal lines on the painted surface, 4 inches apart (Before You Begin).

3 Using a wide, flat brush, paint the window box and molding. Apply two coats, allowing one day for drying between coats and one day after final coat. Keep outside lines as straight as possible.

4 Transfer leaves and flowers to the shower door using a soft lead pencil (Before You Begin). Cluster motifs without overlapping them to create a natural, cascading effect from the window box.

5 Using a soft, round brush, paint leaves and flowers. For contrast, paint designs with two shades of paint. In a freehand style, paint the flower centers a darker shade and add vines to connect the flowers and leaves.

6 To create shingles, paint over the pencil lines with a soft, round brush. Add vertical lines in various lengths every 4 to 5 inches. Slightly wave lines for a weathered effect; remove the tape.

STORAGE
WITH STYLE

At first blush, storage doesn't inspire much decorating excitement. In fact, it is more often thought of as a problem to be conquered instead of a challenge to be finessed. But storage and displays can become integral, attractive components of a room's look and feel. That's what this chapter is about—working with your storage needs to provide creative and attractive solutions. There are a few extra, related ideas here too ... also quick and easy to make, course. We all need to store "stuff." Here's how to do it with style.

DECORATIVE SHELF TRIMMING

Transform utilitarian shelves and add charm with simple shelf trim.

YOU WILL NEED

- ❏ ARTIST'S CRAFT VELLUM
- ❏ METAL RULER
- ❏ PERFORATED PAPER FOR EMBROIDERY
- ❏ TAPESTRY OR EMBROIDERY NEEDLE
- ❏ CRAFT KNIFE
- ❏ GLUE GUN & GLUE STICKS
- ❏ PENCIL

BEFORE YOU BEGIN

Embellishing a shelf with decorative trim requires little skill or time to execute. Simply measure the shelves, choose a pattern, then cut and punch out the design.

Trim Tips

To determine the dimensions of the shelf edging, consider the shelf's width and the items on display. Also consider the depth of your punchwork design.

Measure the thickness of the shelf to be sure that the trim depth will sufficiently cover the board. The overhang pattern on the trim—here it's a zigzag—should begin at the bottom of this measurement. The overhang edge should end well above whatever it is you stored or displayed on the shelf

below. Also measure the length; measurements need not be exact as excess trim can just be cut off.

Enlarge the template (below top) on a copier to the desired width. Then, transfer all the measurements to the artist's craft vellum (below bottom).

Use perforated paper for embroidery, available in craft stores. It is an ideal tool for transferring a dotted design to the shelf paper.

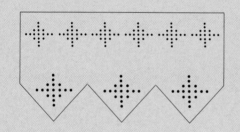

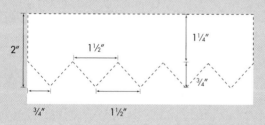

Design Ideas

- Geometric patterns are probably the easiest designs to transfer and punch out of paper. Choose a pattern that complements the design you cut along the bottom edge of the trim.

- Favorite cross-stitch and needlepoint patterns can be easily adapted into punched designs.
- Lightly write a favorite quote or verse from a poem along the shelf trim and punch out with a pin.

138

MAKING DECORATIVE SHELF TRIM

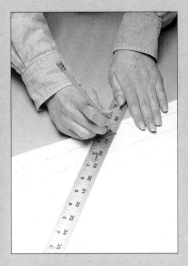

1 Transfer measurements for the trim (Before You Begin) to paper. Draw another line 1 inch from the bottom of the trim. Using a ruler, draw an evenly spaced zigzag pattern between the two bottom lines.

2 Using a craft knife and the edge of the ruler as a guide, cut out the zigzag pattern along the bottom of the trim. Work on a flat, protected surface. Be careful not to cut past the top point of the zigzags.

3 Position a piece of perforated paper over the top portion of the shelf trim; transfer the punched design to the paper with a pencil. Lightly mark the design, being careful not to puncture the paper.

5 Using a hot glue gun, add a few small beads of glue to one end of the shelf edge. Carefully align the trim at one end and alternate adding the hot glue and smoothing the trim in place. Cut off any excess.

4 Lay the shelf trim on a protected surface. With a tapestry needle, begin punching the design onto the paper. Punch only the end of the needle through the paper to keep from damaging the design.

CREATIVE LADDER DISPLAYS

Get the hang of displaying your collections with a ladder design.

YOU WILL NEED
- ❏ PINE LUMBER & DOWELS
- ❏ COMPASS & RULER
- ❏ COPING SAW & CLAMP
- ❏ POWER DRILL & BIT
- ❏ CARPENTER'S GLUE
- ❏ 8-INCH WOOD SCREWS
  & SCREWDRIVER
- ❏ BRASS SCREW EYES
- ❏ DECORATIVE CHAIN
- ❏ S-HOOKS
- ❏ STAIN SEALER & BRUSH

BEFORE YOU BEGIN

Ready-made ladders come in many sizes and shapes, but for a simple version that fits any decor and takes paint or stain well, this custom design may be best.

Ladder Materials

This design (right) and the lengths given are proportioned to fit nicely above most kitchen tables or islands. But you can make modest adjustments in length and width to accommodate your own purposes and space.

• All materials used for this project are commonly available in lumberyards and building supply stores.

• The two rails are 1 by 4 by 60 inches and cut from #1 clear pine. Use knotty pine for a more rustic look.

• The four rungs are 1¼-inch pine dowels, each 15 inches long.

Some Useful Suggestions

When you have lots of treasured collectibles and not enough space to display them, use a ladder. A display ladder offers a wonderfully innovative and versatile device for showing off and storing many such items, particularly in an informal setting. Consider these ideas when searching for unique displays:

• Hung as an overhead rack from which to hang aromatic bunches of drying herbs and flowers.

• Fixed vertically 1 inch out from a wall or the inside of a bathroom door, and the rungs hung with towels or magazines.

• Hung horizontally against the wall of a child's room with the rails and spaces between rungs used to frame and display toys, dolls and stuffed animals.

• Suspended above a work area to hold tools and materials. Hang them by S-hooks over the rungs.

ASSEMBLING THE BASIC LADDER

1 With a compass, draw semicircles at the ends of the two rail sections. To do this, position the compass point equidistant from the sides and the end, roughly 2 inches, and rotate to mark with the pencil.

2 Cut the curved lines with a coping saw. Mark the center of the rails for rungs, starting 9 inches from one end and every 14 inches thereafter. Prop the rails above the work table and drill pilot holes with a 1/16-inch bit.

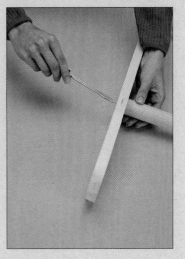

3 Clamp each dowel or rung to the table and drill pilot holes lengthwise at the two ends. Begin assembly along one of the rails by driving an 8-inch wood screw through each of the rail holes and into the matching rung hole.

4 Screw the second ladder rail into position following the same procedures. For more strength, you may wish to add a dab of carpenter's glue to each of the rung ends just before driving the screws home.

5 Fill any rough spots around the screw holes with wood putty and give the ladder assembly a light sanding. Apply a coat of combination stain and sealer to the wood using a sponge brush; let dry.

6 Select one side of the ladder to hang and drill four 1/16-inch pilot holes, each one 5 inches from one of the ends. Screw brass screw eyes into each of the pilot holes. Attach a chain to each eye using S-hooks. Hold the ladder near the ceiling and position the matching hangers. Hang and decorate the ladder.

COLLAGE
UNDER GLASS

Showcase cherished memorabilia in a unique tabletop display.

BEFORE YOU BEGIN

Creating a collage with memorabilia is a wonderful way to spend a cozy winter weekend.

Arranging Memorabilia

• To ensure that the glass lays flat, carefully cut the cover off thick items such as playbills and use only the cover for the collage.
• If you want the messages on the back of the postcards to be seen, photocopy them; then arrange the messages so they overlap with the postcards' pictures.
• Unusual shapes and colors add visual interest to a collage. Cut around the edges of interesting photographic images and trim away unwanted backgrounds.
• Layer, overlap and scatter the items so that the collage has a look of continuity. Avoid covering important parts of the memorabilia when overlapping.
• Once the glass-covered tabletop is complete, choose accessories for display that are in keeping with the theme of the collage.

What to Use

Use this list as inspiration for your own collage:
• Souvenirs from special places or events, such as certificates, wine labels or playbills.
• Old or new photos.
• Miniature watercolors, oils and pencil sketches of family members.
• Travel memorabilia such as postcards, postage stamps, maps and train schedules.
• Dried leaves, feathers and pressed flowers.

MAKING A TABLETOP COLLAGE

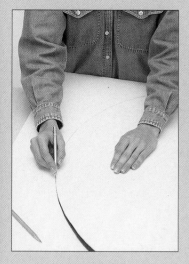

1 Lay a piece of tissue paper over tabletop and trace table's outline. Use tissue paper as a pattern and transfer shape to mat board. Using craft knife, score, then cut mat board along pencil line.

2 Cut around collage items. Trim away backgrounds and cut items into unusual shapes for variety. Place mat board on a flat surface and lay memorabilia within reach so that each piece can be seen.

3 Move items around on mat board to determine ideal display. Lightly mark mat board to indicate placement of each item. Lightly dab back of each item with glue and press flat in position on mat board.

HANDY HINTS

Have the glass for the tabletop cut by a professional. If you are covering a round table, make sure you can tell the glazier the diameter; if the table is square or rectangular, make sure you know the length and width of the top.

TAKE NOTE

The thicker the glass, the less likely it is to break, and the better protected your precious collage will be.

4 Lay mat board collage on top of table. Carefully lift glass and place one edge against an edge of table; begin lowering glass at a 45° angle. When completely flat, adjust glass so that it covers entire tabletop.

COVERED
STORAGE BOXES

Colorful covered boxes store items under wraps and out of sight. But you might not want to hide these beautiful creations!

YOU WILL NEED

❏ BOXES
❏ PREPASTED WALLPAPER
❏ RULER
❏ STRAIGHTEDGE
❏ GREASE PENCIL
❏ SCISSORS
❏ SPONGE
❏ BOWL & WATER

BEFORE YOU BEGIN

Wallpaper totally covers the box to transform a plain container into an attractive patterned one. Start on the outside bottom, go up the sides and wrap into the box.

Measuring for Size

• Measure the length and width of the bottom of the box; then measure the height.
• Cut a piece of paper; the length equals the length of the box plus four times the box height; the width equals the width of the box plus four times the height. If the box is very big, the paper can be cut in two separate strips.
• Use two lengths of paper, lay them out like a cross and paste them together.
• Or cut two lengths of paper, overlap them 1½ inches side by side, and paste.
• Draw the cut-and-fold guidelines (below).

Drawing Template on Paper

Center the box on the wrong side of the wallpaper and mark fold outline with a grease pencil. From each side of the drawn box, measure and draw an area to cover each box side (A,B,C,D, below).

Then extend each area by repeating it (1,2,3,4). The extended areas fold inside the box. Add on the extra X and Y portions to fold around corners and inside so that the seams will not gape.

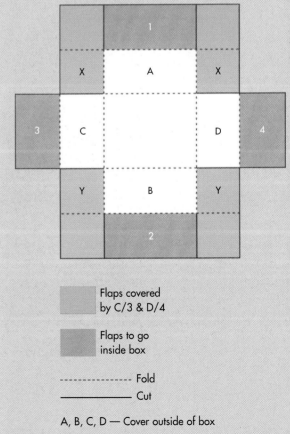

Flaps covered by C/3 & D/4

Flaps to go inside box

-------------- Fold

——————— Cut

A, B, C, D — Cover outside of box

144

COVERING THE BOX

DOLLAR SENSE

Discontinued wallpaper can be a real bargain. Or use ends and pieces left over after wallpapering a room.

OOPS

If the paper tears while smoothing it in place, glue it down carefully with rubber cement, matching the edges. The tear will disappear.

1 Following the pencil guidelines drawn on the back of the wallpaper, use scissors to cut carefully along the outer lines (the straight lines indicated in the diagram in Before You Begin).

2 Use the sponge to dampen the area of wallpaper to cover the bottom of the box. Center the box on top. Smooth out the paper with the palm of the hand, working from the center out to prevent bubbles.

3 Dampen section A and press up to cover the corresponding box side. Then dampen section 1 and press down to the inside of the box. Repeat the process with section B and section 2.

4 With sponge, dampen and press X sections around the adjoining corners of the box and then tuck the flaps down inside the box, smoothing all sides down as you work. Repeat the same process with Y sections.

5 Dampen and fold up sides C and D, pressing to cover the corresponding box sides. Then press flaps 3 and 4 down inside the box, smoothing all the way down to the inside bottom edges of the box.

6 On another piece of wallpaper trace around the base of the box and cut out, making it 1/8 inch smaller all around. Paste inside the bottom of the box. To cover the box lid, follow Steps 1-6.

A RIBBON
LETTER RACK

Crisscrossed ribbons hold photos and cards beautifully close at hand.

BEFORE YOU BEGIN

Padded with batting and wrapped with fabric and ribbons, artist's boards are easily transformed into decorative letter racks. Layer two boards to create an edging.

Cutting Boards and Batting

Artist's boards are available in many sizes at art supply stores. Choose one that's the right size for your letter rack and another one that is slightly larger for the backing.

Lay smaller board on larger one, lining up two of the edges. Draw a line along the two inside edges. Lift off top board and measure out 1 inch. Mark new line with a straightedge and cut on a well-protected surface with an artist's knife (below).

Place both artist's boards side by side on top of the batting and trace a line around the edges of boards. With scissors, cut out the two pieces of batting (below). For a full, plush look, use quilt batting. Use craft batting for a lower loft.

Measuring and Cutting Ribbon

Lay ribbon diagonally across smaller board from corner to corner. Add 2 inches to ends of each ribbon and cut. Mark midpoints on all sides. Lay ribbons from midpoint of one side to adjoining midpoint (right). Add 2 inches to each end and cut.

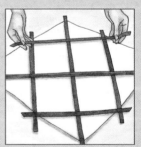

CREATING A LETTER RACK

1 Spread glue on one side of smaller artist's board. Press batting in place; let dry. Lay out one fabric, wrong side up. Place smaller board, batting down, on fabric. Mark 1½ inches all around edges.

2 Repeat the process with larger board. Cut both fabrics following the guidelines. On both pieces, trim fabric diagonally at board corners, close to, but not touching, the edges of the board.

3 Spread a line of white glue around the edge of the fabric. Gently wrap fabric around edges of board to back. Smooth out and press in place. Repeat process with other board. Let glue dry.

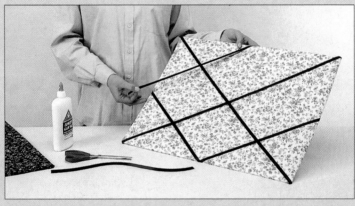

4 Mark four midpoints on fabric on back sides of smaller board. Glue first ribbon in place: attach one edge to the back, wrap it diagonally across the front and glue the other end to the back.

5 To create diamond pattern, glue ribbon on the back at one midpoint and wrap around front to midpoint on adjacent side. Glue in back. Repeat with other two midpoints.

7 Let dry thoroughly. Cover back side of backing board with brown craft paper trimmed slightly smaller and glued in place. Turn right side up and hammer upholstery tacks into rack at edges and at points where the ribbons cross.

6 Liberally apply glue to the back side of smaller board. Turn the larger backing board facedown and center it on the smaller board. Weight with heavy books.

Underbed Storage Drawers

When storage is at a premium, make more room under the bed.

BEFORE YOU BEGIN

Any project is easier to complete when all the pieces and tools are close at hand before you begin. Use the chart below for purchasing all the wood you need.

Purchasing Materials

The measurements below will make a storage box measuring 9½ inches deep by 48 inches long by 36 inches wide that tucks neatly under the average double bed. Measure the space under your own bed before beginning to cut any wood. If this drawer is the wrong size, change the dimensions accordingly.

Materials Required for Drawer

Bottom and Braces	1 piece ¾-inch birch plywood cut 34½ by 46½ inches 2 pieces 1 by 1 common pine cut 48 inches 2 pieces 1 by 1 common pine cut 31½ inches Six 2-inch furniture casters
Sides	2 pieces 1 by 10 clear pine cut 48 inches 2 pieces 1 by 10 clear pine cut 34½ inches 2 handles
Dividers	2 pieces 1 by 8 clear pine cut 34½ inches 3 pieces 1 by 8 clear pine cut 10½ inches 1 piece 1 by 8 clear pine cut 24 inches

Overall Dimensions of Drawer

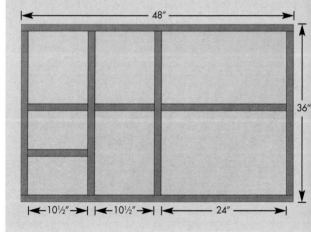

MAKING AN UNDERBED STORAGE DRAWER

1 Glue braces to lower inner edges of drawer sides. For shorter drawer sides, center braces so ends are 1½ inches from drawer edges. Braces cover full width of front and back pieces. Nail braces to drawer pieces.

2 Attach all drawer pieces by first gluing into position, then nailing to secure in place. Drawer front and back pieces should fit onto shorter drawer sides in 1½-inch spaces along edges of side braces.

3 Position plywood base in bottom of drawer so base rests on braces. Make sure base fits snugly—sand edges if fit is a little too tight. Nail base to braces, positioning nails along edges of base.

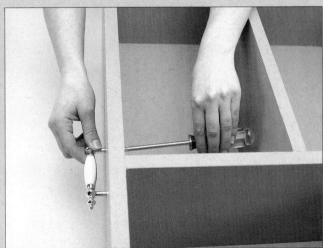

4 Carefully measure and mark lines for drawer dividers using diagram in Before You Begin as a guide. Glue and nail longer divider pieces in place first, then insert shorter divider pieces.

5 On underside of drawer, position casters 1½ inches from sides of drawers and mark screw holes onto base with a pencil. Using #4 nails, make small starter holes. Screw casters securely in place.

6 Prime drawer on all sides, including dividers and base. Paint with latex paint; if more than one coat is necessary, lightly sand between coats. When paint is thoroughly dry, brush on one or two coats of water-based polyurethane; lightly sand between applications. On drawer front, measure and mark handle placement. Install as instructed by manufacturer.

TRINKETS ON FRAMES

A decorated frame is as much of a keepsake as the photograph it holds.

YOU WILL NEED
- ❏ PICTURE FRAME
- ❏ FABRIC
- ❏ DECORATIVE TRINKETS
- ❏ CRAFT GLUE
- ❏ GLUE GUN & GLUE STICKS
- ❏ SCRAP PAPER
- ❏ IRON
- ❏ PENCIL & RULER
- ❏ SCISSORS
- ❏ CLOTHESPIN OR TWEEZERS

BEFORE YOU BEGIN

A strip of plaid fabric cut on the bias—diagonal to the grain—adds interest to an ordinary frame. Find a frame that has a ½-inch inset at the inside edge of the frame. Cut a square of fabric so the diagonal length equals half the measurement around the inset plus 1 inch to turn under.

Making Fabric Strip for Inner Frame

Fold fabric square in half diagonally. Press fold lightly and unfold. Mark 1 inch from both sides of the fold line.

Cut two strips of fabric following center fold line and the marked lines on both sides of it.

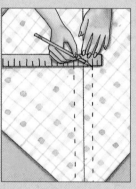

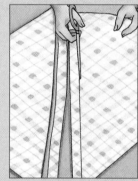

Align ruler on marks and use a pencil to draw lines parallel to center fold. Use longest ruler available.

Fold the fabric so cut edge meets in center on back side. Each edge will be turned under about ½ inch.

DECORATING THE FRAME

1 Apply glue to one side of inset; lay fabric in place. At corner, fold strip back on itself, apply a dab of craft glue, then fold diagonally and glue to next edge. Trim end, fold under and glue. Repeat on remaining sides.

2 On a piece of scrap paper, trace the inside and outside edges of the frame. Using the shape as a template, position trinkets on the paper. Rearrange trinkets until you are satisfied with the placement.

3 Keep the trinkets in place on the template while working, transferring one item at a time to avoid confusion. Locate the position of the largest trinket. Apply hot glue to the frame or back of a trinket.

HANDY HINTS

Hide nicks or chips on old, long-forgotten frames by applying trinkets over unsightly areas to hide them.

DOLLAR SENSE

Solid color fabrics or ones with small prints appear the same whether cut on the bias or straight grain. Purchase only a few inches and cut parallel to the grain when using fabrics that do not benefit from a bias cut.

4 Position the trinket on the dab of hot glue. Hot glue dries fast, so work fairly quickly. If items are small, or if placing glue directly on the trinket, hold the item with a spring clothespin or tweezers to keep glue away from fingers.

New Mirrors from Old Windows

Recycle beautiful old window frames and turn them into charming mirrors.

You Will Need

- ❏ Window frame
- ❏ Mirror glass
- ❏ Wood putty
- ❏ Glazier's points
- ❏ Glazier's putty
- ❏ Paint or stain
- ❏ Picture hanging hooks
- ❏ Sandpaper
- ❏ Putty knife
- ❏ Paintbrush & hammer
- ❏ Ruler

BEFORE YOU BEGIN

Once the scratched glass and peeling paint have been removed, you'll look at old windows in a brand new light.

Removing the Glass

When removing and disposing of the old glass, take precautionary measures and wear heavy work gloves and eye protection at all times.

Hold the frame over a trash can. Cover the frame with an old cloth and gently break the glass with a hammer. Remove the cloth and throw it away.

Remove large pieces of glass by working them back and forth. Use needlenose pliers to remove smaller pieces and the old glazier's points.

Preparing the Wood

• Scrape the old putty and paint from the frame. Fill in any nicks, dents or old nail holes with wood putty (below) and allow to dry completely.

• Measure the length and width of the window openings (below). Take the measurements to a glazier and have mirrors cut to the exact size required.

• Sand the wood thoroughly (below). Wipe down with a lint-free cloth then prime the frame all over.

• Purchase a wood shelf similar in length to the width of the window. If the shelf is made from unfinished wood, prime and paint it as required. If the shelf is already painted, remove the paint and then prepare as previously described for the frame.

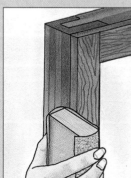
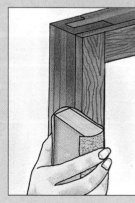

PREPARING THE WOOD

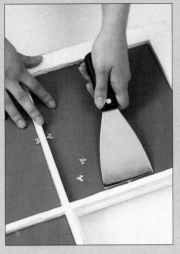

TAKE NOTE

When installing the glazier's points, a small cloth placed on the back of the mirror will protect it from scratches which may occur with the possible slip of the putty knife.

1 Carefully paint the front, sides and trim of the frame. Make sure these pieces are completely covered so that no unpainted surfaces will reflect in the mirror. Let the paint dry. Lightly sand between coats if adding another coat of paint.

2 Position the mirror pieces; handle any sharp pieces with work gloves. Using a putty knife, push glazier's points into the frame to hold the mirrors. Position one point in the center on each side. Use additional glazier's points for larger panes.

3 To keep the mirrors from rattling in the frame, apply glazier's putty to all the edges of each mirror square. For even distribution, use a putty (or caulking) gun or roll the putty into a long, thin rope and apply it to the frame.

5 Be sure to hang the frame evenly—use a ruler or spirit level to make sure everything is straight. Leave sufficient space below the frame to put up the matching shelf. Paint the shelf to coordinate with the mirror and hang it below the mirror using the mounting hardware provided by the manufacturer.

4 Attach picture hangers to the back of the frame and screw strong hooks into the wall. Because mirrors tend to be heavy, consider using wall anchors for extra support. Locate the studs in the wall to support the weight of the mirror.

Board Games on the Wall

Add a folk art look to walls with board games as decorative touches.

You Will Need

- ❏ Birch plywood
- ❏ 1-inch molding
- ❏ Acrylic paints
- ❏ 1-inch foam brush
- ❏ Gold paint pen
- ❏ Painter's masking tape
- ❏ Varnish
- ❏ Sandpaper
- ❏ Cloth
- ❏ Ruler

BEFORE YOU BEGIN

Create folk art decorations for your home by making classic board games for use as wall hangings. Use traditional colors for an authentic antique look.

Measuring the Board Game

A rectangular piece of wood is a good choice for a checkerboard since the longer ends provide space for storing checkers.

Divide the board into a grid with eight squares each horizontally and vertically.

Center the game board square on the wood before drawing the individual squares. The wider ends of the wood should allow for a 3-inch border and the shorter ends a 1-inch border. The finished dimensions are 19 inches by 23 inches. To create a board that's smaller or larger, modify the measurements to the desired size.

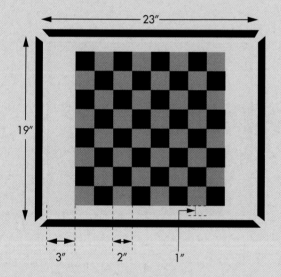

Color Combinations

Instead of painting the board in standard colors, choose colors that match an existing decor. Remember that color squares in opposite corners should match.

Rustic colors such as terracotta, black, golden yellow and brick red have a traditional appeal.

Bright, upbeat colors blend easily with a contemporary setting.

Shades in the same family work well with a monochrome color scheme.

MAKING A WOODEN BOARD GAME

1 Cover whole board front with tape. Using ruler and pencil, draw 16-inch square on tape, 3 inches from long edges and 1 inch from short edges. Divide larger square into a grid of 2-inch squares, with eight across and eight down.

2 Using craft knife, cut out alternating squares of tape to make checker pattern; peel tape from squares. Using foam brush, paint exposed squares with first color. Let dry, then peel away remaining tape.

3 Re-cover board with tape. Using craft knife, cut out unpainted squares to make checkerboard pattern. Peel tape from squares off board; paint exposed wood with second color. Let paint dry; remove tape.

4 Using a medium-tip gold paint pen and ruler, paint along horizontal lines of checkerboard to define squares; let dry. Then, paint vertical lines. When entire board is dry, outline game board border.

5 Lightly sand board randomly for aged, worn effect. Wipe surface clean with damp cloth. Using foam brush, paint entire board with light brown varnish. Repeat when dry for darker finish and a more durable surface.

6 Paint molding; allow to dry. Using hammer and headless brads, tack molding in place around sides of game board. Sand molding randomly for same worn effect as board, then wipe with damp cloth. Finish by painting molding with varnish.

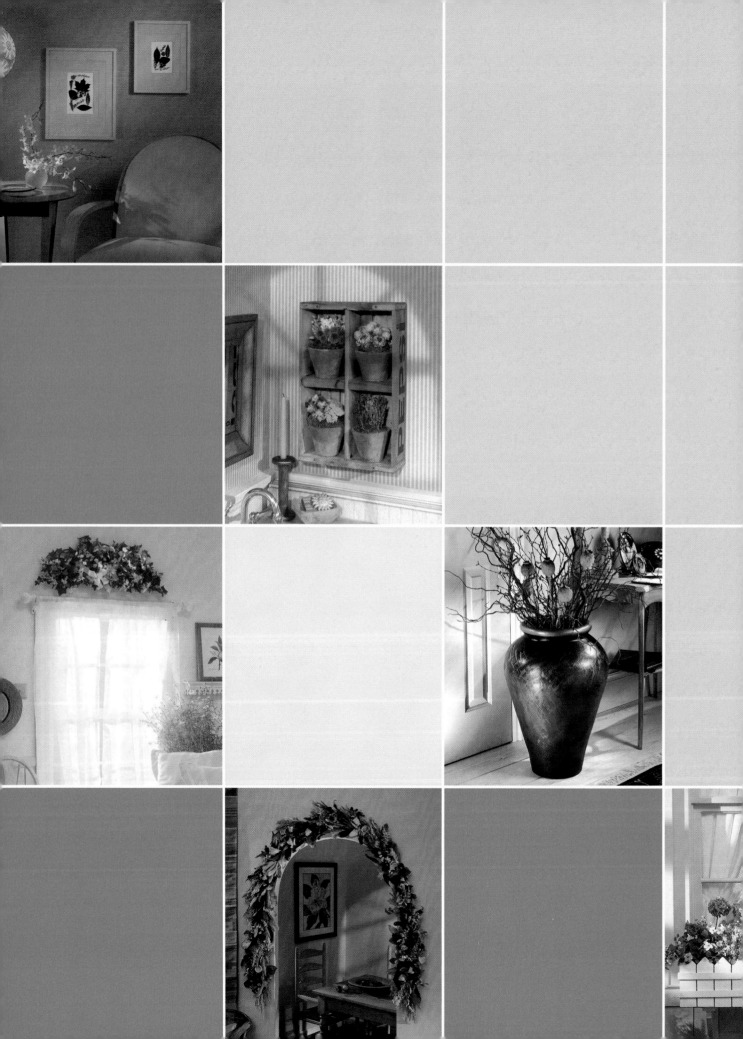

THE POWER OF
FLOWERS

When it comes to decorating, never underestimate the power of a flower. Whether live, plastic, dried or even painted, flowers and floral accents add grace, color and texture to any room's decorating scheme. There's another side to decorating with flowers: The projects—especially the ones in this chapter—are quick and easy to create. Why? Because flowers are so beautiful to start with, you don't have to do that much with them! And that, precisely, is the power of flowers.

PRESSED FLOWER DISPLAYS

To create displays from your garden's treasures, just press flowers.

YOU WILL NEED

- ❏ FLOWERS & FOLIAGE
- ❏ COMMERCIAL FLOWER PRESS
- ❏ BLOTTING PAPER
- ❏ WATERCOLOR PAPER
- ❏ CLEAR-DRYING CRAFT GLUE
- ❏ FRAME & MATS
- ❏ TWEEZERS

BEFORE YOU BEGIN

Some flowers and foliage are more agreeable to drying flat than others. When choosing flowers for pressing, consider each flower's drying time and the ease with which it can be placed under glass or on stationery.

Flower Power

Choose flowers with thin petals and flat surfaces. Avoid fleshy plants and full-petaled flowers.
- Flowers with flat petals, such as pansy, zinnia, larkspur and forget-me-not work well (below left). Also try rose (not in full bloom), daisy, primrose and Queen Anne's lace (below right).
- Various types of foliage that are suitable for pressing are fern, maple leaf, galox leaf, maidenhair fern and magnolia leaf.

Arranging Pressed Flowers

The easiest and safest way to handle pressed flowers is to use tweezers with a blunt end. Pick the flower or petal up by the stem or where the stem has been separated from the flower.

When laying the flowers and foliage on watercolor paper, work in an area only as large as the mat opening. Draw the dimensions on paper, then plan the layout. Also, be sure to choose a frame with enough depth to prevent flowers from getting crushed under the glass covering. When in place, the glass should not touch the flowers.

For a collage effect, add pieces of lace, paper and fabrics to the grouping.

Include memorabilia from a wedding or baby shower, or add snippets of favorite things.

Create a flower study. Place flower heads or petals in rows and columns. If desired, draw a grid between the flowers and use a decorative script to write the names of each underneath.

For a festive look, spray paint dried fern fronds and leaves with different shades of metallic paint.

Celebrate the seasons of the year by creating a series of four arrangements that feature seasonal flowers and foliage.

PRESSING FLOWERS

1 Open the flower press and cover each side with a piece of blotting paper. Lay foliage and flowers on top of the blotting paper, then gently press the other side of the press on top of the flowers.

2 Screw the flower press together as indicated by manufacturer, and leave the flowers in the press for at least two weeks. Once the flowers have dried, carefully peel them from the blotting paper.

3 Arrange the flowers and foliage as desired on a piece of watercolor paper. Using clear-drying craft glue, glue the items in place. Glue one flower at a time, using tweezers to pick up the flowers.

HANDY HINTS

If you don't have a commercial flower press, heavy books will work just as well. Place the flowers between blotting paper, then press them underneath several heavy books. Avoid moving the stack until the flowers are dry.

Apply glue directly to the back center of the petal or leaf. This will prevent excess glue from seeping from underneath the edges.

TAKE NOTE

Keep dried flowers as stationary as possible. Frequent moving before mounting could cause petals to fall off and grasses to shed.

Direct sunlight will fade the flowers. Place them in indirect or low light if possible.

4 Open a ready-made frame and pull out the mats. Lay the flower arrangement on a flat surface, then place the mats and glass on top of the paper. Slide the stack of mats, paper and glass off the surface and carefully place in the frame. Secure the frame.

FLORAL ARRANGEMENTS IN SHADOW BOXES

Frame an arrangement of pretty flowers as a potted wall decoration.

BEFORE YOU BEGIN

Wooden boxes often turn up in unlikely places. Find a good one, then let size and shape determine its use.

In Search of Boxes

Not that long ago, many foods and household items were sold in decorative wooden boxes. Look in kitchen antique and memorabilia stores for specialty boxes:
• Spice boxes, candle boxes, cheese boxes, tea chests.
• Beverage boxes for seltzer, soda pop and fine wines.
• Fruit and vegetable crates, often with handsome labels on each end.
• Cigar boxes.
• Notions display and sewing supply boxes, especially thread trays.
• Printers' trays and dentists' supply trays.

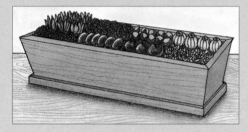

Designing to Fit

Divided boxes (below left) impose their own rules on the design. Experiment with different colors and textures of floral material to arrive at a three-dimensional design that pleases the eye.

Undivided boxes (below right) offer a different set of challenges. In this example, the flowers make the pattern. Insert cardboard dividers on the bias that are half the height of the box sides. Hot glue flowers in place to form colorful stripes.

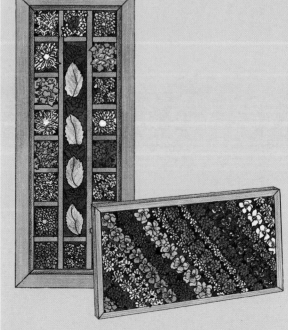

PREPARING THE POTS

1 Using a craft knife, cut blocks of florist's foam to fit each of the 4-inch terra-cotta pots. Let the foam rise about 1 inch above the rim of the pot. Then spread the dried flowers on the table and trim any overly long stems.

2 Arrange one or two types of flowers in the pot, such as achillea and safflower. If the stems are brittle, use a pick to prepare the holes. Place the stems in the pots so they look full and rounded.

3 Continue grouping the dried flowers in the pots. In a second pot, pair purplish blue larkspur with pinkish blue lavender flowers. Attempt to achieve differing combinations of colors in each pot.

4 Cover any florist's foam that is visible under the flowers with green sheet moss. This pot combines dried yellow sweetheart roses with small sunflower heads. In the fourth pot, briza is paired with echinops.

5 Arrange the four pots in an old wooden beverage box. Many such boxes come with dividers in place. If not, make partitions out of wood scraps and distress them to look as aged as the box. Cut matching slits where the dividers meet and slide them together.

FESTIVE FLORAL TABLE SWAGS

A floral table swag makes an elegant alternative to a centerpiece.

YOU WILL NEED

- ❏ ASPARAGUS FERN
- ❏ PLUMOSA FERN
- ❏ WHITE POM-POM
- ❏ PINK ASTER
- ❏ LAVENDER DELPHINIUM
- ❏ PINK LEPTOSPERMUM
- ❏ YELLOW ACACIA
  (MIMOSA)
- ❏ FLORIST'S WIRE
- ❏ SCISSORS

BEFORE YOU BEGIN

There are many different ways to make the base of a floral swag, and it is the base that governs the flexibility and delicacy of the swag.

Making Different Swag Bases

A wire base (a) makes it easy to shape a swag or position it around a table. Cut the wire equal to the desired length of the swag. With separate wire, attach small bundles of flowers and foliage to the base, covering the stems and ends with each successive bundle. Continue adding bundles until the desired length is reached.

A swag of intertwined flowers (b) is graceful and delicate looking, yet surprisingly strong. Simply wire small flower bundles together by placing each successive bundle over the previous stems.

A straw braid or length of raffia (c) makes a more rigid swag. Attach straw or raffia to a stable support. Divide the material into three equal parts and weave the left and the right portions alternately over the center part. Tie the ends securely with a piece of straw, raffia or trim.

Rope (d) creates a very sturdy base, allowing for a full swag that drapes easily and securely. Cover the rope with bunches of wired flowers. Or, allow some of the rope to show for a more casual feel.

Hanging Swags

Drape a measuring tape around the table to see how the swag will be hung. This will also determine the swag's length and width.
• Make it easy to hang swags by forming wire loops at the beginning and end of the swag and intermittently between the ends.

• Use florist's pins to secure the swag to a tablecloth, camouflaging the pins.
• When attaching the swag to a wooden table, use decorative tacks and wire to ensure its security.

MAKING A FLORAL SWAG

HANDY HINTS

If guests will be sitting at the table, make sure the swag allows for comfortable seating and reaching room.

When creating the swags, do not make them so heavy that they cannot be safely secured to the table.

1 Tie off one end of florist's wire to a sprig of asparagus fern. Continue wiring asparagus sprigs together until the desired swag length is achieved. Make a loop at each end of the garland (Before You Begin). Then, create a small bundle of one or two flowers. Twist the stems of the bundle to the fern base with tight loops of wire.

2 Once one or two bundles are attached to the base, wire on some sprigs of plumosa fern. Continue binding small bunches of flowers and ferns in the same fashion, covering the stems of previous bunches.

4 Once the swag is the desired length, cut the wire and wrap it around the stems. Trim the ends of the stems evenly. Drape the swag around the table (Before You Begin).

3 Work toward the end of the swag, positioning the materials in the same direction. Create a specific pattern of flowers or randomly place flowers, taking care to balance both color and texture. Position the bunches so that the width of the swag remains even and the swag is filled with flowers, without it being too heavy to hang from a table.

SILK IVY GARLANDS AND WREATHS

Use silk ivy and flowers to make everlasting garlands and wreaths.

BEFORE YOU BEGIN

Fashion silk ivy into a natural-looking swag that is as versatile as it is beautiful. Add silk berries when celebrating the holidays or silk flowers for formal or country appeal.

The Natural Ivies

Silk ivy comes in many qualities and forms, with some more expensive than others. Choosing better quality ivy generally pays off over the long run in terms of appearance and continuing satisfaction.

All "true" ivies are varieties of the species *Hedera helix*, the common or English ivy. They are characterized by shiny five-lobed leaves that are a solid dark green in color.

Variants may have leaves that range from a simple shield shape to long, pointed stars with edges that are either smooth or rough.

Color is another characteristic that varies. It ranges from green to intriguing mixes of green, white, cream, gray and yellow.

When choosing silk ivy for making garlands, opt for the longest strands. You can always cut them down to size, if necessary. Use shorter "plant plugs" to make wreaths and other decorations, where a shapely result is the prime objective.

Provide texture and brighten the swag by mixing different colors of ivy. In this project, green and variegated ivy is mixed for a fresh, country feel.

To add fullness to the swag, wrap the ivy strands together (below) before securing them onto the base.

Using Live Ivy

To extend the life of fresh ivy and make it more flexible to handle, soak it overnight in a bucket of cool water. After you hang the decorative form, give the ivy an occasional misting with water.

MAKING A DECORATIVE IVY SWAG

1 Trim segments of the green and variegated silk ivy to manageable lengths with shears. Hot-glue the stems to the grapevine base. Arrange them to create a full and textured swag (Before You Begin).

2 Hot-glue the largest of the flowers—the silk dahlias, yarrows, daisies and cosmos— to the base. Take care to insert stems behind the ivy leaves. Work from both ends to make the arch's center the focus.

3 Use the smaller silk forget-me-nots to fill any empty spaces in the decorative arch. Either hot-glue the sprigs in place or pull their stems through the back and secure them around the grapevine.

4 Using wide yellow-and-white gingham ribbon, make a "figure-eight" at one end. Without twisting the ribbon, make a pair of turns over the "figure-eight". Hold the ribbon in the center and make yet another turn. Bind the center of the bow tightly with florist's wire and attach the bow to the bottom center of the base with hot glue.

DECORATIVE TERRA-COTTA POTS

Transform a garden pot into an elegant vase for your home.

YOU WILL NEED

❏ TERRA-COTTA POT
❏ ARTIST'S ACRYLIC PAINT
❏ GOLD METALLIC PAINT
❏ STIFF BRUSH & SPONGE
❏ SCOURING PAD & PLATE
❏ PAINTBRUSHES
❏ BLACK SHOE POLISH
❏ RUBBER GLOVES
❏ STOOL OR LAZY SUSAN
❏ SPRAY VARNISH

BEFORE YOU BEGIN

Artist's acrylic paints are versatile and easy to use—but don't stop there. A touch of gold paint and a little shoe polish will give an ordinary pot greater definition.

Knowing About Pots and Paints

New pots are not necessary for this project, but pots should be clean and free from grease. Scrub old pots with a disinfectant to remove algae and bacteria. Because earthenware absorbs water, leave the pots somewhere warm to dry out thoroughly before painting.

Experiment with materials for applying color as each will produce a different effect. Sponges give a mottled finish—the size of the pattern corresponds to the texture of the sponge. Natural sponges are more uneven than synthetic ones, so their print will reflect this.

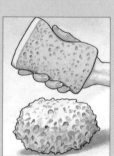

When using spray paint or varnish, hold the can upright about 9 inches away from the surface to be treated. Spray evenly by moving hand from side to side. Do not turn your wrist while working. Always do this in a well-ventilated area and away from children.

PAINTING THE TERRA-COTTA POT

1 Place the pot on a stool in order to work around it without having to move it and touch the paint. Or place it on a lazy Susan to turn it. Brush new pots with a stiff, clean brush to remove dust.

2 Pour some umber acrylic paint onto a plastic plate. Lightly dab the sponge into the paint and apply the base coat over the entire pot. Do not worry if patches of terra-cotta show through.

3 Mix a little white paint into the umber to get a lighter tone. Use the same sponge to apply the paint over the center of the pot, fading the color toward the top and bottom to highlight the shape of the pot.

4 Let the acrylic paint dry for at least 30 minutes. Apply shoe polish around the rim, shoulder and base of the pot with a brush and blend toward the center. Let dry for at least 30 minutes.

5 Neatly highlight the rim of the pot in gold, using a small brush. Follow the manufacturer's instructions carefully—most metallic paints have to be shaken thoroughly to balance color before use.

6 Make rough crosses in gold all over the pot with the edge of a scouring pad. After 30 minutes, spray lightly with varnish.

BRIGHT CHILE PEPPER DISPLAYS

Adorn a doorway with a red hot chile pepper festoon.

YOU WILL NEED

- ❏ CHILE PEPPERS
- ❏ DRIED GRASSES
  INCLUDING: AVENA,
  BRIZA, SETARIA, LINUM
  ATRACXA, ALCHEMILLA,
  LONAS, INDORA
- ❏ OREGANO
- ❏ LEMON LEAVES
- ❏ DRIED ORANGE SLICES
- ❏ WIRE, TWINE & GLUE

BEFORE YOU BEGIN

Available in red, yellow, orange, purple and green and in many shapes and sizes, peppers are among the more ornamental members of the vegetable group.

Pick from a Peck of Peppers

Chile peppers are grown today all over the world, with more than 200 distinct varieties recognized.

In rural Mexico and New Mexico fresh chile pods are tied together in long festoons and hung from roof eaves or on outdoor racks to dry. These striking festoons have become a traditional part of harvest decorations.

But you need not wait for a harvest to spice up a room in your house. Use various types and colors of peppers to create festoons, garlands and wreaths. Keep one in the kitchen so in addition to adding charm to the decor, peppers can be picked for cooking.

For pepper variety, look in produce markets and gourmet shops or raise some of the following in your own garden:

Anchos are heart-shaped, oxblood red fruits, typically 5 inches in diameter, with thickish stems and possessing a flavor ranging from mild to moderately hot (1).

Anaheims are harvested in both immature green and mature red stages (2). Developed and raised principally in California, their typical length is 6 inches and they are mildly hot to the taste.

Habaneros are lantern-shaped peppers that most often grow in greens, yellows and oranges (3). Habaneros are just 2 inches in size, but they are the fieriest of all peppers.

Serranos are small, torpedo-shaped red and green peppers (4). Small and thin, they also are very hot.

Pepper Care

Capsaicin, the substance that makes peppers hot, is an oil found in the inner flesh and seeds of the pod. Handle as follows:
• If desired, protect your skin from possible irritation by wearing rubber gloves.

• Avoid touching hands to your face, especially your eyes, as the oil can cause severe pain.
• When done, wash your hands thoroughly in soap and water.

MAKING A CHILE FESTOON

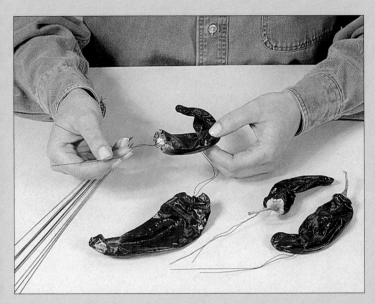

HANDY HINTS

To save time, dried orange slices can be found at florist's shops and craft stores. Or, substitute dried apple slices for the oranges.

1 Measure the doorway to be framed by the festoon and cut a length of cord to fit. Cut a short length of spool wire for each chile, poke one end through the fleshy top of the pod, make a loop and twist the loop closed. Repeat for each pod.

2 Make two small bunches of avena, briza, setaria, lemon leaves, alchemilla and oregano. Using wire, tightly wind the bunches. Continue making bunches, mixing in red chile peppers and remaining materials.

3 Using florist's wire, attach first two bunches, with tips down, to one end of the cord. Continue along the cord, securing the remaining bunches with tips up, alternating from the left to the right side of the cord.

4 When you reach the far end of the cord, wire the last two bunches so that the tips point downward to match the bunches at the opposite end when hung. Hot-glue the dried orange slices at regular intervals. Hang the finished garland.

Bright Chile Pepper Displays   169

PICKET FENCE WINDOW BOXES

Re-create the charm of a picket fence on decorative window boxes.

YOU WILL NEED

- ❏ 1 BY 8 COMMON PINE
- ❏ 1 BY 3 COMMON PINE
- ❏ 1-INCH STRIP OF LATH
- ❏ 2 BRACKETS
- ❏ CONSTRUCTION ADHESIVE
- ❏ CAULK GUN
- ❏ NAILS, BRADS, SCREWS
- ❏ MITER BOX & SAW
- ❏ PAINT & PAINTBRUSH
- ❏ DRILL WITH ¼-INCH BIT
- ❏ HAMMER
- ❏ SANDPAPER

BEFORE YOU BEGIN

To protect the window box from wind and rain, purchase the best-quality pine and coat both sides with outdoor paint or water sealant.

Buying the Wood

- Box width should be as close as possible to the window width. Adjust only to accommodate picket widths.
- This window box is 33 inches wide, 8 inches deep and 10 inches high. The width of your box can vary, but must be evenly divisible by the width of a picket plus ¼ inch for spacing between pickets. Remember that a 1 by 3 board is actually ¾ inch by 2½ inches.
- Example: 2½ inches + ¼ inch spacing = 2¾ inches x 12 (pickets) = 33-inch-wide box. Purchase these lengths:

Box: (33 inches by 3) for base, front and back + 9½ inches x 2 for sides = 118 inches or 10 feet of 1 by 8 pine.

Pickets: # of pickets (18) x height (10 inches) = 180 inches or 15 feet of 1 by 3 pine.
Lath: Measure around two short sides and one long side x 2 = 180 inches or 9 feet of 1-inch lath.

Mounting the Brackets

Use wood or metal brackets to hold the window box in place. Attach brackets directly to house. Mark placement of brackets on house, with each bracket 3 inches from ends of window box. Follow mounting instructions included with brackets.

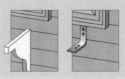

Cutting Pickets

Use pencil and straightedge to mark the centerpoint of each 10-inch strip. Use a miter box and saw to cut a 45° angle off each side of the strip to form the point.

45°

Cer
Poi

45°

MAKING A WINDOW BOX

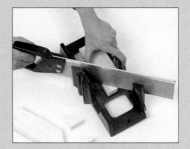

1 Mark eight drain holes on base piece of wood. Position two holes every 6 or 7 inches along length of board. Using a drill and a ¼-inch bit, drill drain holes in base. Sand edges to smooth.

2 Glue one short side of box to base board. Attach side board at right angle, edges flush. Repeat with opposite short side board, then opposite long end. Secure boards with finishing nails.

3 Use miter box to cut each picket piece at pencil markings (Before You Begin). Top of each strip will extend 2 inches above sides of box. Trim tip of peak slightly.

TAKE NOTE

Instead of making the window box from unfinished pine and painting it, use treated wood instead and then allow the box to weather naturally for an attractive rustic look.

4 Sand box and pickets; wipe clean. Sanding creates a smooth surface and helps paint adhere to wood. Prime and paint inside and outside of box, both sides of pickets and lath strips.

5 Use pencil and straightedge to mark correct placement of pickets on front and sides of window box. Leave a ¼-inch gap between each picket. Use construction adhesive and caulk gun to affix pickets securely to window box. Allow adhesive to dry before continuing.

6 Glue lath strips over pickets on front and sides of box. Nail lath strip down with headless brads centered over pickets. Repaint or touch up as necessary.

7 Affix brackets below window (Before You Begin). Place finished window box on brackets. Use pencil to mark exact bracket location and screw holes on inside of box. Drill through box and wood brackets. Attach box to bracket with ¾-inch screws. Coat box in waterproof sealant before using outside.

INDEX